Fr

Earn More

Build on your successes and
take your writing to the next level

Contents

Page

About this book

In 2011 Susie Kearley quit a career in marketing to follow her lifelong dream of becoming a full-time freelance writer. She had no contacts, no real experience in the publishing industry, and no idea whether she would succeed. Yet through sheer tenacity, determination and hard work, she built a solid career as a freelance writer, in the middle of a global economic recession. Today, she works for some well-known publications and earns a living from her writing.

In this book, Susie discusses her approaches to getting published and answers many of the burning questions asked of any freelance writer:

- How much money do writers make? How much do *you* earn?
- How can I generate more income from my writing?
- Where can I find the best opportunities in freelance writing?
- How can I learn from rejection and increase my chances of success?
- How do I break into magazines and newspapers overseas?
- Do I need an agent? What can they do for me?
- What's it like working with a small press book publisher?
- What are the biggest challenges to a sustainable freelance career, and how can I overcome them?

This book discusses writers' average earnings and the many challenges facing someone following a freelance career. It explains how to generate income from feature articles, blogging, books, photography, and content creation for business. It details the money to be made from associations that pay out secondary royalties on your articles, photographs, and books. It also looks at record keeping and organisational skills - essential requirements once your workload reaches a certain level.

This book is written for those writers who've seen modest successes in publishing, to help them take their writing to the next level. It will help anyone looking for new inspiration and insight, who wants to earn more from their writing.

There are many beginners books on the market. This book is different. It focuses on making a regular income from writing. It doesn't go into great detail on the basics like how to pitch, because that's covered in lots of other books, including the author's first book, *Freelance Writing on Health, Food and Gardens*.

Part 1 focuses on different ways of making money from your writing.

Part 2 looks at working for magazines around the world and discusses the things you need to think about when you write for overseas markets.

Part 3 looks at opportunities in book publishing, a day in court, professional indemnity insurance, marketing, social media and writing as therapy.

Part 1: Make Money Writing

Perhaps you're already a freelance writer, but you're part-time, the economic outlook is challenging, and you need guidance and inspiration to take your writing to the next level of success? This book is designed to help you grow from modest successes, to generating a higher income from freelance writing.

In Part 1, we explore different markets for your work, look at new approaches to generating income, explore how to monetise your blog, and look at what writers earn. There's a big debate going on about writers' pay with some arguing that the rates offered by publishers are too low and will damage the industry in the long term. In Part 1 we look at writers' average earnings, explore the arguments and give you the information you need to form your own opinion.

Chapter 1
When one door closes, another one opens

In 2011, I quit a 15 year marketing career to throw myself headlong into freelance writing. It was a childhood dream. I'd not had any journalism training, but I did have a solid background in marketing, which stood me in good stead for this progressive career change. I had a reasonable knowledge of how publishing works, having produced publications and worked with a range of contributors, designers and print companies in my marketing roles. I'd had to write, edit and produce documents, source high-resolution photographs with appropriate permissions (or take them myself) and comply with the law relating to publishing.

Back track to the 1990s, when I tried to break into magazine journalism in my spare time - it was a disaster. I tried for years, while working in dead end day jobs, and studying on courses that were available at the local college. They didn't offer journalism. After years of disappointment, I finally gave up and followed a career in marketing instead.

Marketing enabled me to unleash my creativity in some areas, like graphic design, but I felt very constrained by corporate culture, organisational politics, and the apparent need to make everything sound so official, stuffy, and boring! My attempts to make dull newsletters more interesting, were usually met with displeasure. I longed to have the freedom to be more creative.

I worked in the education sector for a while, constantly fire-fighting against bad press and incompetent teaching. On the upside, I had the opportunity to study the full range of professional marketing qualifications with the Chartered Institute of Marketing, which was no small feat. But deep down I wasn't cut out for the corporate life.

I was a creative writer – I wanted to make things honest, interesting, and funny - draw on the hazards of life in my writing, not try to cover them up as part of a PR stunt and hope no-one noticed! I wanted to write colourful stories about life's ups and downs, highlights and disasters. I wanted to write raw, painful, ridiculous and hilarious true stories, and I wanted to dabble in fiction. None of this would have been appropriate in organisational communications.

Then the recession struck and there were redundancies. By 2011, having already seen many colleagues leave, I was facing redundancy too. They offered me a decent voluntary severance package and the alternatives looked bleak, so I took it.

Considering my forward career options, I liked the idea of working for a charity because I wanted to do something worthwhile and meaningful. Interview after interview ensued, but no charity was interested in employing me. There was always someone with more relevant experience. As the severance money slowly trickled away, I wondered if I'd made the right decision.

Then after a short period covering maternity leave in the local council offices, I made a life-changing decision to follow my lifelong dream of becoming a freelance writer. I'd lost confidence in the idea in my teens and 20s when rejection after rejection confirmed that my dad's bleak opinion of my talents was correct: I'd never be a writer. My creative ambitions were crushed. So it was a huge leap of faith to step back into the mindset of my artistic self, and aim for the stars.

It was a short spell in a temporary marketing job that opened my eyes to the opportunities in freelance writing. It made me realise that I really could live the dream and didn't have to be tied to the corporate life with all its constraints and disappointments. The role that led me to this conclusion was a disaster, but the lessons I learnt in that short-lived position, changed my life.

I set myself up as a freelance writer in the middle of the worst global recession in decades. I set up a website, uploaded the few small items of published work that I had to my name, registered as self-employed with the tax office, and declared that I was a freelance writer. For weeks, I spent all day, every day, pitching ideas to magazine editors, and as the weeks passed, and the rejections filled my inbox, I wondered if I was kidding myself.

Then suddenly I received two commissions within ten minutes of each other from two different gardening magazines, and a third commission came in from a military history publication. I was on a roll!

I jumped around in delight, whooped with excitement, and then sat down to begin writing them. I'd presented myself as a professional freelance writer. There was no room for imperfections if I wanted repeat business from these magazines. That was the start of a career that led to me becoming a full-time freelance writer, working for dozens of magazines around the world.

Back in 2011 when I started out, I felt like a fraud - claiming to be a professional, with little published work to my name - but that feeling didn't last long. I quickly identified some niche titles that I hadn't considered before. One of my earliest commissions was for Fly Past – a military aircraft magazine. It was an historical tale of a war hero. I didn't need expertise. I just needed a good story, an interviewee, and some pictures.

When I thought more laterally about what I could write for different publications, and really pushed myself, I did have expertise that their readers were interested in, even if it wasn't in their core subject. I had qualifications in marketing, management, nutrition and psychology. I wrote a lot on nutrition, and did a lot of interviews in those early days, and I still do a fair bit of that today.

As the work started to flow in, I was in my element. Within a few months, my collection of published work was looking much more impressive. By the end of my first year, I was generating regular repeat work for the same publications. Then I started to expand overseas, working for magazines in other English-speaking countries and succeeding there too.

My new business went from strength to strength, and while the money in the early years was poor, compared to my previous employment, I had all the benefits of being able to manage my own time and workload, pick my assignments, and crucially, I enjoyed my work. I didn't have to comply with other people's annoying rules and preferences, and I could slot leisure activities into my working day when it suited me.

Then early in 2013, I saw a social media post by Compass Books looking for authors to write on specialist topics. I made an informal enquiry about writing a book on freelance writing, specialising in health, food, and gardens.

They looked at my submission and asked me to write the first chapter for their consideration, but I didn't have time and it ended up at the bottom of my pile because I was too busy with magazine work. Eventually, they offered me a book contract based purely on the portfolio of work displayed on my website. I clearly had the skills and know-how to write the book, so they offered me a paid book deal, without even seeing the first chapter. I was amazed. I thought getting a book contract was supposed to be really difficult! It seemed too good to be true, and I read through the contract carefully. I'm unlikely to make my fortune, but it still held massive appeal. Writing books had been my dream since I was about eight years old! I signed the contract and then found the time to fit writing the book into my evening schedule.

Within three years of starting my writing career in the middle of a recession, I had a heavy workload and had had a book published. The salary crept up year after year, and I was runner up in a Writer of the Year Award in 2014.

So how do I feel about the challenges of redundancy now? I'm absolutely delighted that it happened to me. If I hadn't faced redundancy, I may never have had the confidence to leave my steady job and realise my ambition to be a freelance writer.

It took huge perseverance, inner strength, and determination to keep going in those early months, when I was pitching ideas all day and getting rejection after rejection, but it paid off.

I now see that when one door closes, another one opens, and challenges that seem insurmountable at first, may actually be a blessing in disguise. Now I try to look at the opportunities hidden behind some of life's challenges, instead of worrying about the future.

Not only am I fully employed as a freelance writer, covering a wide variety of really interesting topics, but I've escaped the drudgery of corporate life and managed to get a book deal on the strength of my day-to-day work.

My dreams are coming true, one by one. Now that I'm on the right path, I have so many projects I want to complete and so many books to write. I've learnt so much by researching my articles in the past few years, it's incredible. I am now inspired, have a real sense of purpose and a passion for my work.

Chapter 2
Writers' pay - The big enigma

The first question everyone asks of a professional writer, is "How much do you get paid?" Even among those who are too polite to ask, it's invariably a question that everyone secretly wonders. Fortunately, it's something that the Author's Licensing and Collecting Society are interested in too. The ALCS is a body that collects secondary royalties, such as photocopying fees, on behalf of writers and authors and distributes them once a year to its members. It also lobbies on behalf of writers for better pay and conditions.

In 2014, the ALCS published its latest report on writers' earnings. A total of 2454 writers responded to the survey, including those working in the fields of journalism, authorship and feature writing, as well as other areas of the writing profession. The respondents included members of the ALCS, the Society of Authors, the Writers' Guild of Great Britain, and the National Union of Journalists. Some were full-time, some were part-time, and some were occasional writers with another profession.

The results of the survey, which were compared to a previous one conducted in 2005, paint a picture of falling earnings and economic hardship among writers, but it is perhaps overly gloomy and not as clear-cut as it may seem at first glance.

Critically, the researchers didn't ask writers about the number of hours they worked. 'Professional authors' were simply defined as, 'those who spend the majority of their time writing'. Upon clarification of this with the ALCS, I was told, "The survey did not capture hours worked, rather the percentage of working life spent on self-employed writing. 'Professional authors' are those spending 50+% of their time writing. The majority of respondents to the survey were 'professional authors'."

According to the report, professional authors earned £11,000 per annum on average from their writing. This is a typical median figure for respondents, of whom 88.5% had another source of income. It suggests that the vast majority of professional authors surveyed were writing part-time. An income of £11,000 doesn't strike me as too bad for a part-time job, but it obviously depends on how many hours they're putting in and what other benefits they're enjoying from the experience.

Also, 29% of all respondents were over the age of 65, so many of these may be relying on their pensions as their primary income source. Now I could be wrong, but I'd be surprised if many of the over 65s are putting in a 40 hour writing week.

The exact split between 'professionals' and other writers is not clear - neither are the hours worked, or the definition of 'working life' - which for some people will mean much longer hours than others. However on balance, I suspect that the survey figures are distorted by a high number of part-time writers. Back in 2005, when the ALCS last conducted this survey, the economy was booming and professional authors were earning £12,330 per annum on average (a comparable figure of £15,450 today). However, in 2005 40% of professional authors earned their income solely from writing - which suggests that 40% were full time - or at least working longer hours than they do today. When you work longer hours, you can generally expect your earnings to be higher.

The bigger question perhaps, is why a higher proportion of this year's respondents have gone part-time and developed secondary income streams? Or why more part-timers have responded this year. Are the full-time writers too busy to participate?

I suspect some writers have developed new income streams because it's getting tougher and tougher to secure a full-time workload as a writer. The economy is challenging and every industry is diversifying - just look at the agricultural industry and you'll find wind farms, solar farms, holiday lets, campsites, and ostrich farming.

In today's competitive environment, diversification can benefit writers too. Having photography skills, an address book to die for, a willingness to do whatever it takes, or a penchant for illustration, could go a long way to furthering your writing career!

The report continues, "Professional authors are typically earning less than the Minimum Income Standard (the acceptable standard of living) in the UK." However, this only takes into account their income from writing. It doesn't take into account the 88.5% of professional authors that have a second income/pensions. When you take those into account, it doesn't look quite so gloomy.

My personal experience of writers' pay is mixed. Yes, I've seen some magazines go out of print during the economic downturn, and I've seen others cut their fees. But there are also those that have grown, some that have increased their print regularity from quarterly to bimonthly, and completely new publications that have started from scratch and succeeded despite the economic challenges. I've seen publications increase their circulation and I've seen pay go up - and back down again!

There is no doubt that the industry is competitive, and competition drives down fees, but I can't help feeling that the rise of writing hobbyists, writing workshops, and institutions like the Writers' Bureau over the past 20 years, has perhaps swayed the survey figures towards part-time earnings.

The good news is that the creative industries in the UK are thriving: the ALCS report says, "Statistics produced by the Department of Culture, Media and Sport in 2014 show that the creative industries are now worth £71.4 billion per year to the UK economy (over £8 million per hour) and the UK is reported as having 'the largest creative sector of the European Union'."

The point they make is that writers should get a decent cut of this: perhaps a fair point. The upside however, is that the creative industries are growing, so there are increasing numbers of opportunities to be taken up by creative professionals. Don't give up or take too much notice of the doom and gloom.

It's perhaps appropriate that the final heading in the report, is 'Adapt and Survive'. Writers who are flexible and adaptable, who learn new skills and put themselves forward for opportunities, might be pleasantly surprised to find out just how much they can earn.

I still believe it is possible to make good money writing. Yes, times are challenging, but that statement applies to almost every profession at the current time. Those who work hard, put in the necessary hours, and persevere, can be well rewarded for their efforts - not just in monetary terms either. They get a sense of achievement and wellbeing in doing something they love and being paid for it.

Perhaps I should conclude that I'm a full-time writer and I'm earning quite a bit more than £11,000 per annum. I'm not special. You can do this too. Follow me on social media for more hints and tips to assist your writing career: @susiekearley on twitter, or www.facebook.com/susie-kearley-writer

What else the survey said

As well as analyzing writers pay, the ALCS survey looked at writers' contracts and found that 69% retained the copyright to their work, and 57% signed contracts with a rights reversion clause - this enables authors to reclaim their rights when their book goes out of print. 70% of those who used the reversion clause went on to earn more money from their manuscript.

Just over 25% of respondents to the survey said they'd self-published, with a 40% return on investment, and 86% said they'd do it again! "Digital publishing is now the third largest sector in terms of financial importance for writers," says the ALCS report. Only a small proportion of respondents had received income from digital publishing, but it's a growing area that includes ebooks, online magazines and newspapers, as well as audio-visual productions.

The lesson? There are opportunities out there for tenacious writers - whether it's in digital publishing, magazine articles, books, or maximising the resale rights on your earlier work. Persist, adapt and survive.

An alternative perspective from the Society of Authors

When I asked the Society of Authors' Chief Executive, Nicola Solomon, for her views on the report, I briefly explained my suspicions: "My view is that the £11,000 figure represents a part-time income and that the reality for full-time writers is not as bleak as it appears."

She didn't agree.

Nicola went on to explain her perspective in some detail: "It is true that many of those in the study who self identified as 'professional authors' have another job but that is because they cannot earn a living from writing. A 'professional author' for this study is a person who 'dedicates the majority of their time to writing'. The survey found that only 11.5% of PROFESSIONAL authors earn their living solely from writing. In 2005, this figure was 40%. That is extremely concerning because it shows that even those who dedicate most of their time to writing can no longer make a living from writing and that the proportion who can, has fallen very rapidly. We believe that this is because authors are not receiving a fair share of the profits from book publishing- particularly in relation to digital. While authors' earnings are going down generally, those of publishers are increasing. Retailers like Amazon are also pressing for a larger share of the profits. Authors are the only essential part of the creation of a book and are asked to do more and more in terms of publicity but are receiving lower advances and a smaller share of the profits. If unchecked, the rapid decline in the number of full-time writers could have serious implications for the breadth and quality of content that drives the economic success of our creative industries in the UK.

"Amazon says that it only seeks a lower price for its customers but, as we have seen with supermarkets and milk production, constantly driving down prices can mean that producers can no longer economically create their goods.

"Whilst the amount of money authors are earning from digital publishing has increased, overall, the survey results show that authors' incomes are falling in real terms. The typical annual income of professional authors has fallen to £11,000 - a figure far below the level identified by the Joseph Rowntree Foundation that is required to achieve a socially acceptable standard of living (£16,850). This decline is set against the increasing wealth generated by the creative industries, which now equates to a staggering £8 million per hour.

"The picture is much worse when you look at those for whom writing isn't their main profession. In 2000, the typical annual income of 'all writers' was £8,810 in real terms, whereas in 2013 this figure had fallen to £4,000. The ALCS findings state that average author incomes have fallen by almost 30% in the past decade. Creative Industries Council data shows that UK creative industries are growing at 5× the broader GDP growth rate.

"Our members are certainly 'feeling the pain'. Not only are incomes falling but the terms being offered to authors seem to be worsening. The Society of Authors continues to fight for fair incomes and fair contract terms for authors as it has been doing for the last 130 years". She attached a 10 page paper of recommendations for authors' contract terms.

Not wishing to cast too much of a negative stance on the current situation for writers, she also had some encouraging words to share...

"Despite the challenges, I do not think the situation is entirely negative for authors. First, self-publishing means that authors have real and viable alternatives to the traditional publishing houses. This has proved empowering for many and lucrative for some. Second, other forms of funding are emerging such as crowd funding and the SoA's own Authors' Foundation Awards. Third, digital provides a range of opportunities in new media that were unimaginable only a few years ago. And fourth, and most important, we see a real appetite for stories and for reading, which is not diminishing despite competition from other media. One of the duties of writers is to support reading in all its forms: to support libraries, literacy, bookshops and books in prisons - to name but a few of the campaigns the SoA has supported this year."

Further reading on this topic from the Society of Authors: www.theguardian.com/books/2014/jul/11/traditional-publishing-fair-sustainable-society-of-authors

The National Union of Journalists

John Toner, National Organiser for Freelance and Wales, at the National Union of Journalists says: "As opportunities for writers in traditional media have greatly reduced, there is no doubt that more writers are struggling to maintain their income levels. Many professional writers need an alternative source of income in order to do this.

"New media publishers often expect writers to work for very little, and in some cases for nothing at all. The results of the ALCS survey are not surprising when considered in this context.

"The figure quoted is a median, which means some writers will be earning considerably less. There are, however, freelances who continue to earn high incomes even in these hard times."

Final thoughts

I do think that writers' pay across the board has fallen and people are having to work harder for the same money. I've had to take cuts, and fees are being trimmed back in almost every sector of publishing.

I think competition has increased a lot too, which is driving down fees, but I still manage to make a decent living as a full-time writer - and I started my writing career in the middle of a recession, with no contacts. It is possible to make a living as a writer if you have the willpower and tenacity to succeed - and then the dogged determination to sustain your position in an increasingly competitive environment.

What do I earn?
My income for the first three years' trading was as follows...

Year 1
From July 2011 to April 2012, I completed commissioned assignments to the value of £15,000 working full-time hours. A lot of this time was spent pitching ideas to publications, and I was taking time out for interviews until I was sure that the writing income was sustainable. I only got paid £12,000 because some of the work was held back by publishers for publication the following year. It is usual to get paid on publication, not on acceptance. There were deductions for expenses and then I had to pay income tax and National Insurance.

Year 2
From April 2012 to April 2013, I completed commissioned assignments to the value of £21,000 working full-time. However, I only got paid £19,000 because some of the work was held back by publishers for publication the following year. Some magazines went bust without publication of, or payment for, my work. There were deductions for expenses and then I had to pay tax and NI.

Year 3
From April 2013 to April 2014, I completed commissioned assignments to the value of £31,000 working full-time. However, I only got paid just under £26,000 because some of the work was held back by publishers for publication on a later date, and some magazines went bust without publication of, or payment for, my work. Others changed their minds after sitting on articles for long periods, then decided not to use them and not to pay me.

Fortunately, that's a small minority, and most publications do pay eventually. That's the nature of the business - but as my workload increases, I'm getting more choosy about who I work for. I invested in some pricy equipment in year 3, so after expenses, my actual earnings were rather lower. Then, of course, I had to pay tax and National Insurance.

Year 4
From April 2014 to April 2015, I'm on target to complete commissioned assignments to the value of about £31,000 again, working full-time. However, to date, I have only been paid £8,000 because I am writing this in January 2015 and most of my pay comes in one to two years after the work has been completed. By the time this year's tax return is due, in January 2016, I should have received most of the income - and expenses will be lower this year.

If you're used to a fat salary, then my income may look a little bleak on paper, especially in the early years. However, it's not so bad. Remember that the outstanding articles will mostly be paid for eventually, and the expenses incurred during the course of my self-employment are not without benefits. My financial investment has enabled me to get a decent camera, lenses, a better computer, software, and other essential tools for my work.

It's also reasonable to expect the early years of self employment to be relatively low paid, while you build your workload, grow your client list, and invest in equipment to take you further. I'm very pleased with what I've achieved over the past four years, and I'm well equipped to earn good money from writing in the future.

However, I am increasingly finding that publishers are holding articles for long periods, and some then change their minds, without offering kill fees. This is affecting my income and making me look seriously at diversification: publishing more books, maximising income on photography, and looking at business writing as a more reliable source of regular income. I also need to continue pitching widely and winning new clients in the newspaper and magazine industry. There's no room for complacency in a line of work that's as competitive and changeable as freelance writing.

Chapter 3
Different ways to make money as a writer

The world of publishing is changing fast as readers increasingly turn to the internet for articles and news, and ebook publishing revolutionizes the world of books.

What does this mean for writers? More opportunities online and fewer in print perhaps? That's certainly an emerging trend, but it's not all bad news for the traditional publishing world. Some specialist print publications are bucking the trend with growing readerships. Other former print publications have switched to online publishing. Magazines that have moved to digital-only format in recent years include Easy Living and Paranormal magazine.

Across the industry, budgets are being stretched, so as a freelance writer it pays to think broadly about opportunities in the modern world.

How then, in such a difficult environment, can you make money as a freelance writer? For me, the key has been tenacity. I just kept going - on and on. I kept pitching until I wore the editors down and they either blocked my email address or gave me work. I never gave up. I sat at my computer day in, day out, pitching ideas to publications all around the English-speaking world. Tenacity is very helpful in this line of work.

There's also an obvious requirement to be a good writer, to have flawless spelling and grammar, an endless flow of ideas - and to be able to deliver articles that meet the needs of the readership, in the correct style for the publication.

If you're targeting the traditional press, you should read a lot of magazines and newspapers to understand the markets and the different styles adopted by different publications. If you're targeting online opportunities, check out the unique styles and characteristics of those publications too.

Magazines and newspapers
Most of my work is in magazine and newspaper publishing. There's a whole section on magazines later in this book, but the key to growing your workload in magazine or newspaper publishing, is thinking

outside the box and identifying the publications that would be interested in your specialist interests and knowledge.

Work up fresh angles to appeal to the readers of publications for whom you'd like to work. These might include interviews with interesting characters, research on new technologies and innovations, or relevant news and features.

Look around you for inspiration and you'll find there are feature ideas everywhere you go - at work, at play, in the news, and in the people you meet and the places you visit. A dogged determination and persistence are two important keys to success in this market.

One important aspect of working for magazines and newspapers, is that it's necessary to write a really good pitch. Write something short but compelling, that will make editors want to assign you to do the work.

Do you have a really great feature idea - preferably one that they can't do in house? Do you have a new or unusual angle on an old story? Or an interviewee lined up who can add real value to your piece? Summarise your proposal in a couple of paragraphs and make it attention-grabbing and current. Why should the editor run it in a forthcoming edition? Try to include a newsworthy or seasonal 'hook' that makes your topic particularly relevant. Do you have photographs that will make the article more appealing?

Be aware of the lead times that different magazines and newspapers work to. Some publications work up to a year ahead, so if you're pitching something timely and topical, you need to bear that in mind. Try to get ahead on special anniversary dates, and pitch seasonal articles well in advance. My biggest customer works at least six months ahead, but often commissions articles a year ahead. This means I can be writing Christmas articles in the spring and summer articles in December. Think too, about what samples of your work might impress the editor, and be ready to send some over on request.

Identify which similar or relevant publications you have worked for in the past, and explain why you're the best person to write the article. Editors are very busy people, so keep it succinct, and if your proposal grabs their attention, you might have an assignment on your hands. Good luck!

Internet opportunities

Opportunities to write for online publications, e-magazines, guest blogs, and websites are abundant. There's an insatiable appetite for material online, but for the most part, it doesn't pay very well. That's why most of my work is in print publishing. However, if you need to build up your portfolio or raise your profile, then writing for online publications can be worthwhile, and if you're savvy, there is money to be made online. I've won a few assignments where the client paid very well for specialist articles to go on their website.

Contributing to blogs can also help to promote your book, build your reputation, and raise your profile. Get it right, and you can make good money blogging - the revenue comes from advertising, affiliates and sponsorship packages. Blogs that attract a lot of hits can bring in decent advertising revenues and may increase the sales of your books, so keep writing, and one thing might lead to another.

I've recently come across a website worth looking at if you're interested in freelance writing jobs www.freelancewritinggigs.com. There are plenty of opportunities for web writers and bloggers advertised on this site, as well as opportunities in editing and in print.

I talk about blogging in more detail in the next chapter, and it's definitely an area worth looking into if this kind of writing work appeals to you.

Books

Many writers aspire to having books published and an increasing number are doing it themselves. Whatever your perspective on this, writing books is usually less profitable than writing articles for the press, but books can still be a great way to improve on your writing prose and generate a modest income. Of course, if you *really* succeed in this area, then the financial rewards can be considerable! Part 3 of this book looks at book publishing.

Maintain high standards

One thing that keeps editors happy in all these areas, is a commitment to high standards. It means, broadly speaking, that those who have published your work before, will be pleased to use you again. This might seem obvious, but it can be really easy to think your first draft is brilliant and hit the 'send' button. The truth is, a first draft is rarely brilliant. Make sure your work is up to scratch before you submit it. Get it proof read and if the editor requests alterations, bend over backwards to get it right. This applies whether you're working for magazines, book publishers, or online.

Fees

The fees in freelance writing are so variable that it can be difficult sometimes, to know what to charge, or whether to accept a commission. For the most part, with magazines and newspapers, the fees are set and non-negotiable. I received a commission from an Australian publisher recently, and when I worked out the exchange rate and conversion fees to sterling, it barely seemed worthwhile. However, I managed to do the job reasonably quickly, by starting with an article of mine that had been published in the UK, and revising it for the Australian market. It hadn't been published overseas, so there was no conflict.

In the last few days I've pitched an idea to a magazine and been offered £20 to write it - I laughed. I've never been offered that little before! I'm currently trying to establish how long it will take to do the work. If I can turn it around in an hour, I'll take it. If it's going to take all day, I won't. I think it's fair to say that I won't pitch to that magazine again. I'm not interested in publications that only pay £20.

As a general rule, I spend more time on the articles that are well paid, than on the articles that are poorly paid, and if I know a publication doesn't pay very well, I only pitch ideas that I can do reasonably quickly. The best paying publications always get first refusal of my best ideas. And if the pay is really bad, I don't pitch to them at all once I know the rate.

When you're pitching for work on a freelance writing website and you're asked to provide your fee, estimate the amount of time that you'll need to complete the task. Then multiply it by how much you want to make per hour and provide a quote based on that figure.

So what's the best way to make money?

For me, it's all down to perseverance. I have income streams from magazine publishing, specialist newspapers, photography and books. Spreading yourself widely is worthwhile financially, and it helps to build your reputation. Think broadly about the opportunities in publishing today and dabble in different aspects to see what works for you.

Chapter 4
Make money with photography

One thing I didn't expect when I started writing for a living in 2011 was to learn the value of photography. Being able to offer good photographs to accompany your work can add considerable value to your submission. Whether you're writing about travel, gardening, recipes, or real-life, publishers do value having imagery supplied with the words. It can make the difference between an article being accepted or rejected. In fact, for some publications, the imagery is more important than the words.

That's why, in my second year of trading, I invested in a professional camera, some decent lenses, and enrolled myself onto a photography course. Today, more than half my articles depend on good photography. Back in 2011, I was struggling to get the necessary results with a compact camera.

Many people think you can legally copy photographs off the internet to illustrate your work. In most cases, you can't. Firstly, you'll be breaching someone's copyright, and secondly, the photos won't usually be high resolution enough for a print publication anyway. Some tourist boards and visitor attractions will send you high resolution photographs free of charge in return for good publicity.

Image Libraries
Many image libraries exist to supply photographic images to people and businesses who need them. Most charge for the use of a photograph, but there are a few free resources that are worth knowing about. For example, if you need images of British locations then you may find what you need at: www.visitenglandimages.com or www.visitbritainimages.com. Registration is simple and free. You must credit the photographs correctly. Check the terms and conditions to ensure you comply.

There are also some generic photo-libraries that allow you to use pictures free of charge, but do check the terms and conditions on each, because often the commercial use of the photography is forbidden.

Some sites that, at the time of writing, do allow free downloads for commercial use include:

- www.rgbstock.com
- www.pixabay.com
- www.morguefile.com
- www.freerangestock.com
- www.freestockphotos.biz
- www.dreamstime.com/free-photos

These are membership-based sites. For some of them, I'd be a bit wary of sending the photos to magazines, as the websites rely on their members, from all around the world, understanding and respecting copyright laws. Any photographer who genuinely owns the copyright to a photograph, is much more likely to have made a high resolution copy available for download if he wants other members to be able to use it. A low-resolution photograph, therefore, may be more risky. You may want to check with the individual who has uploaded it, that it's definitely their photo, before you use it commercially.

Always check the licence terms and credit the photograph correctly if that is a requirement. Some sites charge for higher resolution files, but let you download a small image free, to use on your blog or website. Another website that offers photographs free of charge for non-commercial uses, such as blogging, is www.photl.com.

Do it yourself

Despite all these resources, it can still be tricky finding the perfect shot and you can't beat improving your own photography skills. Then you can take the pictures you really need to illustrate your work. Providing your own photographs avoids any problems with incorrect credits (magazine designers often forget the credits!). When you take your own photographs, you can feel confident that you're OK legally, and you can claim royalties from DACS Payback too. This is explained shortly. Be assured that there are many benefits to be gained from taking your own photos, not least the pleasure of getting good results!

Chapter 5
Make money blogging

The traditional role of writing articles for print publications is changing as the digital age transforms the world of publishing. If your feature writing isn't generating the income you'd hoped for, it's worth looking at other ways of making money from writing - such as blogging. As the traditional publishing industry struggles in the economic downturn, and tries to adapt to the digital age, let's look at the role of blogging and where it sits alongside more traditional forms of writing. Is it really possible to make good money from it?

"Yes it is!" say professional travel bloggers, Nick and Dariece, from 'Goats on the Road'. They earn $2500 (£1528) on a good month and spend 15-20 hours each week working on the blog while they're travelling. Not a bad fee for blogging about your holidays!

Sophie Lizard, the founder of 'Be a Freelance Blogger', says she earns $100 (£61) per hour and works about 20 hours per week, which suits her nicely.

Amy Lynn Andrews from 'Blogging with Amy' makes $500 (£305) a month from blogging 4-6 hours a day. It's not her primary source of income - her blog is a marketing tool that generates additional work in design and consulting.

Ruth Holroyd from 'What Allergy' makes £400 a month from her blog, which she writes in her spare time. She is also a full-time self-employed marketing manager in the allergy and free-from foods industry.

Monetising your blog
Bloggers often make a living doing what they love and writing about it. Nick and Dariece use the income generated by their blog to pay for their continuing travels around the world.

Ruth from 'What Allergy' started out blogging about places to eat for people with multiple allergies because she suffers from severe multiple allergies including nuts, dairy, soya, wheat, latex, nickel and dust. The blog became so successful, that it's now expanded to include her experiences with allergies, eczema, and to discuss a wide range of allergy-related topics. The blog was started five years ago and now tops 100,000 unique visits every month. It won the Free-From Food Award in November 2014.

So is blogging really a feasible alternative to selling articles to publishers? Well it depends how successful you are, but ultimately, yes, it can be. What you earn varies enormously from month to month and your success obviously depends on your blog's popularity, your search engine rankings, and your loyal following. If you're dedicated to it, and you build this up over time, anything is possible!

Advantages of blogging over writing for magazines

With my traditional magazine feature writing, I'm still waiting for articles I wrote over two years ago to be scheduled! Fortunately my slowest client pays on acceptance, but I have another client who's a front runner for second place - and they pay on publication. I can see that some of my work will be outstanding for years before I get paid.

In delightful contrast, blogging offers instant gratification. You can self-publish instantly, and you don't have all the aggravation of trying to find a publisher for your work. You don't have to chase up invoices or experience frustrating delays in payment, because it's all automated, based on the number of visits to your blog. If you write a compelling blog, you can literally start earning straight away.

As more magazines go digital, there is a definite trend towards online publishing, and the boundaries between traditional publishing and e-publishing are becoming blurred. In some cases, e-books for example, it can be quite hard to tell whether the work has gone through a professional publishing house, or whether it's self-published.

Blogging is an excellent way to promote yourself and your books, or your other creative works. If your blog captures your readers' interest and imagination, you can quickly gain a decent following that can result in increased visibility, increased income, and increased sales of your books.

How do professional bloggers make their blog pay? Successful bloggers use affiliate links, advertising, sponsorship, products and merchandise, and linked promotions to make their blog pay. Some even ask for donations to help keep their blog going.

There's a publishing revolution taking place right now. Blogs have exploded in popularity over the past decade and are starting to present serious competition to printed magazines. The blog revolution is transforming article publishing. It's a bit like e-readers opening the floodgates for self-publishing.

The upside of the digital age

While the world of publishing may seem tough and quite overwhelming when you're trying to get an article accepted or a book deal, blogging gives you an instant audience – especially if you have a good social media following.

The internet revolution has also created an insatiable appetite for new material and there are paying opportunities for writers to operate as guest bloggers, or regular paid bloggers for publishers.

The ladies' writing magazine, Mslexia, employs guest bloggers for a period of three months. They want people to blog about their writing challenges, offering hints and tips for writers to learn from. The Guardian also has extensive blogs, but the easiest approach is to set up your own blog and build your own following through social media. You might be surprised by just how successful it is.

Ten point plan

Here's my ten point plan for making money from article writing, outside the traditional channels:

(1) Advertise on your blog

This is perhaps the simplest way to start making money online. If you use a site like Blogger or Wordpress, you can very easily apply to display adverts on your blog. Then, if your application is accepted, you will receive a fee based on the number of visits to your blog. The more people who view your blog, the more you earn.

(2) Use affiliate links

Some professional bloggers use affiliate links to monetise their blogs. Nick and Dariece, from 'Goats on the Road' say, "We have affiliate links throughout the site to travel companies. If our readers purchase a visa, accommodation, or travel insurance through one of these links, we receive a commission. Our readers don't pay a cent extra, so it's a win-win for everyone!"

As Ruth's *What Allergy* blog increased in popularity, advertisers started to contact her. She now participates in affiliate schemes from www.clickbank.com on relevant topics. There's a link from her site to her chosen affiliate site and when someone clicks through and buys from the affiliate, Ruth receives commission. With the combination of relevant advertising, affiliates, and sponsored articles, Ruth makes her blog pay.

Amy Lynn Andrews says affiliate links generate the most income from her blog. One affiliate partner that might be of interest to writers is Hive bookstore, who offers anyone with a website, the opportunity to become an affiliate. They say, "Hive offer 6% commission on book and stationery orders and 3% commission on eBook, DVD, Blu-ray and CD orders". This assumes that the original referral comes from your website or blog as part of their affiliate programme.
www.hive.co.uk/hive-affiliate-programme

(3) Post promotional features
Allow selected advertisers to write articles for inclusion on your blog. 'Goats on the Road' do this, without actively promoting the features. They say, "We only highlight these articles to our readers if we believe the content is outstanding."

(4) Get sponsorship
A sponsorship package is similar to advertising but it's more like a partnership agreement where the sponsor pays you a fee, and in return you offer them a package that includes significant exposure on your blog. If there's an obvious sponsor-candidate linked to the kinds of things you're blogging about, then getting sponsorship could be a good way to generate more income.

(5) Sell stuff
Some bloggers sell products such as ebooks or health products. Whatever you have to sell should be related to what you're blogging about. A soft persuasive approach usually works better than a command to 'buy my stuff', which can just be annoying.

(6) Be a freelance blogger
Blogging sites like 'Suite 101' or 'Love to Know' also offer a variety of blogging opportunities enabling writers to cover the subjects that interest them.

(7) Promote yourself as a writer
Blogging indirectly helps to generate income by creating interest in your wider work – whether that's books, feature articles or other writing projects. Greater interest often leads to increased sales.

(8) Write tweets!
Building a twitter following is a great way to promote your blog. It can increase your hit rate dramatically. There's also a big market out there for people to write tweets and Facebook updates for companies that don't have the time or inclination to do it themselves. It may not be your first choice of writing assignment, but it can help pay the bills while you chase the more fulfilling work. You can use your own Twitter account to promote your own blog.

(9) Publish your previous work
If you're looking for content to get your blog started, then why not take extracts from articles that you've already had published and post them onto your blog? If you have a book, and your publisher's contract allows it, you can publish extracts onto your blog with the aim of increasing book sales.

Useful links
www.goatsontheroad.com
www.beafreelanceblogger.com
www.bloggingwithamy.com
www.hive.co.uk/hive-affiliate-programme
www.whatallergy.com
www.clickbank.com

Chapter 6
Writing for business and commerce

Some writers offer copywriting services to businesses who require marketing content for brochures, corporate newsletters and other materials to help them engage with clients and prospects. This might not be everyone's cup of tea, but the benefits of this kind of work are that you are more likely to get paid quickly, the pay can be quite good, and if your clients like your work, it could lead to regular work and regular income. This might make it easier to follow your real dream of writing that best selling novel, or selling features on your favourite consumer topics.

Content Cloud is one such platform that's worth a look. It's relatively new and was developed to bring together content creators - writers, journalists, marketers, PR professionals and artists - and the businesses looking to employ them.

It's dubbed as, 'the new online content marketing solution where specialist content professionals secure work directly from firms, agencies and publishers producing content in the business sector'.

I first came across the opportunity through newsletters from Press Gazette - a great resource to keep you up to speed with all things going on in the world of journalism. You can sign up to Press Gazette newsletters and when you read about some of the financial challenges facing some publishers it might shed light on why some of your clients take so long to pay!

Back to the business opportunity: The promoters of the new online facility say, "Content Cloud is open to experienced, quality journalists, editors, researchers, photographers and illustrators looking to create high-end editorial for big brand companies. It ensures quality by letting users offer sealed bids for tendered work and guarantees payment within 30 days of submission."

That 30 days payment is a real bonus - take it from someone who still waits years for payment, only sometimes to find that an editor changes his mind and doesn't use the article at all. Content Cloud is free to join and if you have either a passing interest in business writing, or an interest in doing it as a sideline to help bankroll your real passion, it's worth considering. It's free to join and use for all

Content Creators, and I made £600 from assignments commissioned by clients on this website within the first few months of joining.

You can register here: www.thecontentcloud.net/contentdesk/register/contentcreator.

Or take a tour online at www.thecontentcloud.net or www.youtu.be/tuz-Ej3OVYY.

It's also worth noting that there are other, more established, sites where freelance writers can bid for a variety of projects, from ghost writing to business-related writing work. They include www.elance.com and www.guru.com. The opportunities are mixed - some are poorly paid - but I know some people do get good work from these sites by being selective.

Writing marketing literature

Other writers specialise in certain topics or do freelance marketing for a living, which involves a lot of content creation. Writing for business can pay well and has the bonus of a regular income. If you have specialist industry knowledge, you're in a good position to approach companies, or marketing agencies, working in that sector.

Of course, it always helps if you're passionate about your topic - this will shine through in your work and keep you interested in what you're doing.

If you're interested in marketing, then the Chartered Institute of Marketing courses are highly respected and offer you a good grounding in business marketing.

The marketing principles you learn can be applied to marketing your books and promoting yourself as a writer too. There are many benefits to be gained from having a good understanding of marketing when you're self-employed, entrepreneurial, and needing to market yourself to potential clients on a daily basis.

Furthermore, many small marketing agencies employ writers to assist with clients' projects. If you're interested in this kind of work, why not contact your local marketing agency to find out if they use freelance writers and whether you're a good match for the kind of work they do?

Part 2: Writing for Magazines

I'm assuming that you already have some experience in pitching article ideas to magazines, but for those who would benefit, here's a quick recap: email the features editor / commissioning editor / managing editor and explain in one or two paragraphs what your feature idea is, why you're the best person to write the article, why the publication's readers would enjoy it, and provide a 'hook' - a link to an upcoming event to make it current and newsworthy. Make the idea really compelling and with any luck, you'll have a commission!

When you get into relentless pitching and regular commissions, it helps to be really well organised. When I write a pitch, I keep a copy of it and record who I've sent it to, so that when I'm uninspired, I can return to my previous ideas and see if I can use them to generate more work. I have hundreds of pages of ideas that I recycle with every new season.

I'm really busy with work now, but getting into this position was tough. Initially, I only had about 1% hit rate which meant I needed to pitch 100 ideas for every success. The hours were long - I worked intermittently in the evenings and on weekends, as well as dedicating my weekdays to it. On the upside, that commitment not only paved the way for my freelance career, but it gave me permission to get distracted, or go for walks, in the daytime and not feel too guilty about it!

This section looks at writing for magazines, highlighting different sectors and the freelance opportunities in each of them. Hopefully you'll find some inspiration in the following pages. There are some exercises to help you think through the opportunities.

Chapter 7
Build up your workload with niche titles

My recent commissions have included articles for The New Humanist, Bowls International, The British Philatelic Bulletin, H&E Naturist, ASCL Leader magazine, Practical Reptiles, Woman Alive, and Cage and Aviary Birds. These are all niche titles, serving very specialist markets. Niche publications offer some of the best opportunities for new writers, or for those just looking to expand their client base.

If you have specialist knowledge, or expert interviewees, then niche titles can be well worth a look. The biggest challenge with small press magazines is identifying those that pay. If you go too niche, you'll find that many of them don't pay - they ask hobbyists to write for free. If your goal is simply to be published, that's fine. If your goal is to create a portfolio of work, leading on to better things, that might be beneficial too, but if your goal is to make money, then you need to weed out the payers from the non-payers and target your efforts accordingly. There's no easy way to do this, except ask. The magazine's website or the Writers' and Artists' Yearbook may indicate payment rates, but often they don't.

Think about what you know, your qualifications, and areas of expertise. Are you an engineer? Then perhaps you can write for Civil Engineering magazine. Are you a psychologist? Then perhaps you can write for Psychology Today. Are you a paranormal investigator? Perhaps Nexus or Fortean Times are more up your street. Do you practise crystal healing? Then you might find Rock and Gem magazine would like to hear from you.

Are you a Christian? Athiest? Pagan? Muslim? Spiritually undecided - or perhaps you believe in fairies? There are magazines for them all, all keen to hear from writers offering unique insights on these specialist topics.

There are thousands of publications out there, all needing content, and the key is to find those that suit your writing style and your interests, where you can add value, perhaps more-so than other would-be contributors.

Consider opportunities in local publications such as the Archant Life magazines, which might be interested in local stories about new businesses opening up in your area or people with interesting stories to tell. They always enjoy tales of local heroes and people who have overcome adversity.

I've done a lot of work for light hearted, popular spiritual publications, and remarkably, learnt a lot of British history from researching ghost stories! In order to reveal why the restless spirits of royals and aristocrats roam stately homes and castles across the UK, I've had to delve into the past, learn their stories and tell their tales.

I've researched the murder of the Princes at the Tower, the Wars of the Roses, Henry VI dying in the Tower and Richard III. I've got a better grasp of Henry VIII's wives and the life of Queen Victoria. On that note, let me tell you a little more about writing for spiritual publications...

Chapter 8
Writing for the spiritual markets

"We don't do realism" said the features editor of a popular spiritual publication. I'd just offered to cover Spontaneous Involuntary Human Invisibility for the magazine.

On the face of it, the story appeared to be right up their street. It was an interview piece with US paranormal investigator, Donna Good Higby, who says the solar system is changing to bring about a new planetary power grid, like meridians in the human body or the leylines on earth. The theory gets weirder, but is interesting – she asserts that deep meditation can create a higher consciousness, which takes you to a higher frequency, causing spontaneous human invisibility.

I was going to link it up to tales of astral planes and the scientific theories of parallel universes. The magazine prints tales of goblins and fairies, angels and demons - all true, of course - so it seemed spot on. However, it was apparently, too scientific for that particular publication.

Despite their aversion to realism, over the years, I've sold a lot of articles to spiritual magazines. Maybe that's a reflection of my own little world, where nothing is impossible and fantasies become reality if you work hard enough. I've sold articles to Kindred Spirit magazine on alternative medicine and sold ghost stories and fairy sightings to 'real life' publications.

One of my earliest commissions for a spooky tale, was for Paranormal magazine, covering the haunting of Hughenden Manor in Buckinghamshire, which according to some sources, has its own resident ghost: Victorian Prime Minister, Benjamin Disraeli.

I rocked up at the Manor House. There was a guide on the door.

"Have you seen this ghost? Can you tell me about the paranormal disturbances?" I asked.

She laughed, "What ghost?"

I explained what I'd heard about a haunting, paranormal investigators, a visit by the Ghost Club, and the phantom in the woods. She turned to her colleague. "Do you know anything about a ghost?"

"Someone saw a Victorian figure in the office once," she offered, "He just disappeared into thin air!"

Now we were getting somewhere. That particular visit was fairly fruitful in the end. The tour guide at the estate knew more about the ghost, and told me that some visitors had said they'd seen the fire pokers jump around by themselves. She was sceptical about the visitors' motives, but it didn't matter. It made a good tale, and I was eventually put in touch with a clairvoyant who had experienced Disraeli's presence in the drawing room.

It's great when everyone gets into the 'spirit' to help you with your 'true' ghost story - but a little trickier when they look at you like you're mad. I had this problem at Bodiam Castle, and Missenden Abbey. At Bodiam the property manager told me it was a lot of nonsense - but then added that some visitors do report a strange cool aura (that made it into an article). At Missenden Abbey the manager, after he'd stopped laughing, conceded that some workmen on site reported strange things happening at night.

Sometimes you just can't get people to talk about ghosts, and then you're reliant on internet blogs of people's spooky experiences. However, when you need to get out there to get quotes and photographs, you really have no choice but to go and ask those awkward questions!

I consider it a bit of fun. I've sold a fair number of ghost stories to spiritualist publications, and there's always an increase in appetite for these tales at Halloween.

Many spiritual publications aren't interested in reality. But it helps to understand which publications are interested in the truth, and which are really just indulging their readers' spiritual fantasies. For publications like Take a Break's Fate and Fortune, and Chat It's Fate, you need people with fantastical stories about ghosts, poltergeists, spiritual healing, and angelic intervention. It doesn't matter if they're a bit mad - all that matters is that they tell a good yarn and are happy to pose for photos!

These magazines are led by incredulous tales of the supernatural. They often reject anything that presents a scientific or logical argument, but they love anything to do with Wicca, spiritualism, Eastern religions, new age culture, and hauntings. Beware, if you offer them something about paranormal investigations, you'll probably get a knock back. It might just be deemed too scientific. Try Haunted magazine instead.

The market for tales of the strange and miraculous, and sometimes spooky, is wide and diverse. Paradigm Shift, Faeries and Enchantment, Horoscope, Haunted, and New Dawn (Australia), all take slightly different approaches to their exploration of the spiritual realm.

In this sector of publishing, anything goes. You can write wholeheartedly about your dead grandmother leading you from the grave to follow a more fulfilling path in life, or the alien abduction experienced by your best friend. They love this stuff. You can cover spontaneous human combustion and astral travel. No-one will bat an eyelid. You can talk about the weird and miraculous, and the mind-bogglingly radical. For some magazines, the weirder the story, the better.

A similar type of publication to the 'real life' magazines, are the trendy women's magazines that focus on the spiritual side of life, as well as health and beauty. To sell a 'true' story of spiritual healing, or divine inspiration to these publications, it may help if your interviewee is beautiful. I've had a number of proposals rejected and I got the impression that it was because my interviewees, who all had good stories, were simply not beautiful enough (the stories were rejected on sight of the photos)!

These publications are all about beauty, horoscopes, psychic powers and spells. They include Soul and Spirit, and Spirit and Destiny. They carry true life stories of women who have had remarkable experiences with a spiritual twist, and they might include tales on spiritual healing, developing your sixth sense, or divine weight loss. They are also interested in celebrities, clairvoyance and angels.

Others with a focus on health, healing, clairvoyance and spirituality include Caduceus, Kindred Spirit, and Prediction. They all cover strange alternative therapies and spiritual healing techniques. Sometimes they'll touch on nutrition and run better substantiated health articles too.

If you prefer to write for a more serious publication on issues of this nature, then there are publications that do in-depth reports on all things weird. Fortean Times, Nexus, Dot Connector, Mindscape,

Paranormal, and Fate (USA), are all much more interested in the science behind strange phenomena, as well as cutting-edge and highly controversial debates about health, conspiracy theories, doomsday predictions, UFOs, aliens, and anything else that's just plain weird. They too, cover spiritual possession, hauntings, and other paranormal phenomena.

Finally, don't forget the pagan publications which include Pagan Dawn, Pentacle Magazine and Witches & Pagans. They cover pagan beliefs and activities including the gods of nature and the power of spells. On another level, they are quite down to earth, with concern for environmental issues, and the morals of capitalism (or lack of them). They promote an ecologically friendly way of life, and are into calm and meditation, as well as Druidry, Wicca, and their inherent pagan theories and practice.

The fiction market for spooky tales is also diverse. Black Static and The Edge are among those that specialise in dark tales of the supernatural, gothic horror and dark urban fiction. If you fancy writing horror fiction, short stories for these markets are a good way to flex your brain muscles, and practise your skills in preparation for that best selling horror novel you've been intending to write for the last 20 years.

Spiritual publications enable writers to unleash their imaginations into the limitless world of the supernatural, maximise their creativity, and explore theories on the cutting edge of science and paranormal research. But evidently, not all of them!

Exercise

Do you know anyone who claims to have seen a ghost? Do you know anyone involved in paranormal psychology? Or do you have special insight into the world of the occult? How about crystal healing and alternative therapies? The more spiritual, the better.

This sector is worth checking out if you can answer 'yes' to any of these questions. If you don't have contacts, or specialist insight, then you might still be able to research topics or do interviews with people who do. Jot down any angles you can think of for this area, and see if you can work up some good ideas.

Chapter 9
Writing for lifestyle magazines

Lifestyle magazines are the broadest, biggest selling sector in the industry, with dozens of women's magazines, plenty of men's magazines, and some cultural titles, designed to appeal to both sexes. It's such a huge market, with such diverse coverage of different topics, that it's an obvious starting point for any writer, but be warned - it's flooded, very competitive, and can be hard to break into.

Now if you've been writing for magazines for a while, it's likely you've already had one or two things published in lifestyle publications. Some of them take readers' contributions, so if you're not having much luck on the editorial side, you can always hit the readers' slots - I'm not too proud to do that, and have had lots of stories, letters, holidays and photographs published in readers' slots over the years. Some of them pay quite well too!

As my writing career has developed, I've done increasing amounts of work for lifestyle magazines. I cover health topics as a qualified nutritionist, and do interview pieces with people who have interesting life stories to tell. I've sold many fascinating stories to women's magazines including a tale of sudden blindness, an interview with a Butlin's Redcoat, dozens of health and nutrition pieces, and a few true life tales of my own.

Among the keys to success in this sector are a good network of contacts willing to share their stories, a total lack of inhibition to talk about your own life - especially the embarrassing or juicy bits, and a shed-load of determination to knock down doors, which on the face of it, might seem closed.

Expertise in a lifestyle area is also beneficial of course - perhaps fashion is your area of expertise, perhaps you're a relationship counsellor, or perhaps you have a fascinating hobby that you could draw upon to help you create articles for this sector?

Lifestyle magazines are always on the lookout for human interest stories. They also run articles on health and fitness, beauty, fashion, shopping, celebrity, and travel. There are hundreds of different topics you can cover for lifestyle publications, and there is inspiration all around you in the places you visit and the lives of your friends, family and acquaintances. In fact, when you've squeezed every bit of potential from friends and family, there's no shame in making new friends with interesting stories so that you can sell their tales too (with their permission of course)! You might get into fee splitting at some stage, but hey, it's all work, and if you can rework the piece later to sell another similar story, then you both earn double the money!

Lifestyle is not a particularly easy sector to break into, but it's diverse, and for that reason, inspiration for this sector is quite easy. All around you, people are living interesting lives and have amazing stories to tell. It's just a question of identifying the right story for the right market, writing a fantastic pitch, and then pitching the idea to editors until someone says 'yes'! The downside? Getting a 'yes' could take years!

However, hopefully it won't take years. Sometimes you can bag a commission very quickly. When you get a commission, deliver a fantastic story and with a bit of luck it'll be easier to get more work with the same editor next time you have a great story looking for a home.

Exercise

What's your preferred topic for lifestyle magazines? Are you a retail guru? A fashion fanatic?

Try writing a pitch to a magazine of your choice, on a lifestyle topic explaining why your idea is topical and why you're the best person to write the piece. Perhaps there's an interviewee you can offer who will add value to the article.

Chapter 10
Writing about pets, animals and wildlife

There are hundreds of magazines specialising in animal topics, from BBC Wildlife to Horse magazine. I've written for Popular Fish Keeping, Practical Reptile Keeping, Dogs Monthly, Guinea Pig Magazine, and Cage and Aviary Birds, but animal magazines aren't the only ones interested in animal stories.

I've sold stories about red kites on breeding programmes to regional magazines, stories on a crane breeding programme to a heritage magazine, a zoo keeping article to a travel magazine, and articles on wildlife hospitals to general interest magazines.

Try to foster good relationships with the editors of magazines and you might get the opportunity to interview readers who've got in touch about their projects. One of the articles I wrote for Practical Reptile Keeping was about a reader who had turned his garage into a reptile house. The editor assigned me the task and later asked me to cover exotic pet insurance too.

On another occasion, I did an interview with the reptile keeper at Cotswold Wildlife Park in Oxfordshire, who told me all about their pair of breeding alligators, the new batch of babies, and the challenges of working with reptiles at the Park.

If you're into horse riding, stable care, or horse racing, then there are dozens of horse magazines, including ones specifically designed for teen readers and sport enthusiasts. 'Eventing' is a publication focusing on horse trials. They commission articles from freelancers and cover everything from industry gossip to rider profiles, event reports and opinion pieces.

Among my earliest published works were a couple of articles for Dogs Monthly, about Hearing Dogs for the Deaf, and how to train your dog to dance. They also publish veterinary pieces, health articles, breed features, and canine diets. If you come up with some good angles, then the specialist dog publications can provide good opportunities to cover tales about talented dogs, rescues and rehoming, special canine diets, or community projects like pet therapy.

There are also cat publications offering similar opportunities. Cat World regularly advertises for contributors with specialist knowledge and expertise on feline topics. Could that be you?

Most animal magazines are interested in veterinary expertise so it's useful to have a specialism or interview contacts in this area. I've interviewed specialist vets for features in the past and reported on the veterinary treatments used for all kinds of rabbit health issues.

Wildlife publications are many and varied, and often require a degree of expertise, a brand new angle and some stunning photographs, but even if you're not an expert or a wildlife photographer, if you have excellent contacts, great interviewees, and can lay your hands on suitable photographs - with the permissions to use them - these publications too, can be worth a punt.

One of my writer associates has a unique approach to writing about wildlife. He tackles mysteries and legends, covering wolves that are rumoured to roam forests and sea creatures that are the stuff of legend - like the Loch Ness Monster but usually more obscure. He's into cryptozoology, and finds unusual angles on wildlife topics by drawing on this fascination to provide unique angles to his stories.

He also covers obscure endangered species, writing profiles about the creatures, interviewing experts, and looking at the challenges they face in their natural environment.

There are many wildlife publications including BBC Wildlife, Discover Wildlife, and the WWF World Wildlife Magazine, to name just a few. There are also opportunities to write for www.wildlifeextra.com online, and to target non-wildlife publications with wildlife stories if you can find a suitable match.

For example, environmental and sustainability magazines might be interested in wildlife an conservation stories because the two topics are related.

Exercise

Think about any contacts you have in the world of animal care or wildlife conservation. Would they be willing to be interviewed? Write down some ideas on animal topics and try to identify some publications that might be interested in covering these stories.

Chapter 11
Writing on history, nostalgia and genealogy

There are dozens of history magazines on the market including BBC History, History Today, American History Magazine, Military History Monthly, Britain at War, Ancestry, Family Tree, Who Do You Think You Are. The list goes on and on.

Most of the specialist history magazines want expert historians to write for them, but if that's not you, don't despair. You can still write about historical topics, but you might need to select your markets carefully, then come up with some amazing interviewees and unusual angles, or perhaps both!

Magazines like Best of British are full of nostalgic articles, looking back on recent history with interviews, museums, and war stories. They take a wide range of story ideas but have a big backlog of articles and won't necessarily use your article, even if they accept it.

This is not ideal for the writer who needs to be paid in the forseeable future, nor is it suitable for articles that have an imminent expiry period. However, the broad scope of their published works makes this magazine an interesting one to consider. It's also worth noting that they have a readers' column for memoirs, and publish quite a large number of readers' memories every month. It's a paid slot, albeit modest, so if you want to tell your story, you could try this section.

Some of the military history magazines will accept war memoirs too. I wrote regularly for one of them, lining up interviewees for each monthly issue and telling individuals' unique stories of their varied roles in the Second World War... until the magazine discontinued the column. If you have a compelling war story, magazines like Britain at War or Fly Past might be worth a punt.

There are other markets for war stories if these magazines don't bite your arm off. I sold an article on a war-time nurse to Family Tree magazine when they were considering running regular readers' features. Some of the genealogy magazines are interested in historical features and run articles on life in the 1800s and 1900s, when many of the reader's relatively recent ancestors would have lived. What was life like for a maid, a workhouse master or a chimney sweep? It can make compelling reading.

Other historical features, such as pieces about Victorian workhouses, appear in all sorts of magazines from kiddies' titles to regional magazines. If you have special expertise in an historical topic, you could perhaps cover it for History Today or BBC History, but if you don't, there's nothing to stop you pitching ideas to a generalist title. Tales following the lives of the poor and destitute in Victorian England have appeal to all sorts of publications if you target your markets carefully and pitch your ideas skillfully.

One of the more interesting aspects of my past that I sold to an historical magazine was a piece about my own ancestors. I'd never given much thought to my ancestry until I was speaking to my dad about the work he'd done on our family tree. I knew we had some distant relationship to Lord Byron, the poet, but I didn't know the details. Finding out about it was an interesting process, if a little long-winded!

It transpires that my great, great grandfather was Henry James Byron, the actor and playwright, second cousin to Lord Byron, the famous Victorian poet. I am also related to Samuel Solomon — one of the most notorious, and successful, quack doctors of all time.

This second relationship was a complete revelation - he's an interesting character who sold Solomon's Cordial Balm of Gilead across the world in the 18th century. It supposedly contained magical secret ingredients, including pure gold.

Now because I'm into natural health, which my dad thinks is a load of baloney, I think he might hold the view that some of Samuel Solomon's charm has rubbed off on me. I however, prefer to think I take after the literary masters, the Byrons, and hope I can do them justice in my writing career!

These two characters - Byron and Solomon - formed the basis of a story I sold to Best of British magazine. However, the research into my ancestry also revealed that I had an ancestor who was a workhouse master, and conversely, one desperately poor ancestor who was forced to live in a workhouse until her death. There were all kinds of interesting characters mentioned along the way, and some of these people might provide stories for genealogy magazines, nostalgic or historical magazines.

Exercises

Think about your own family history. What are the interesting elements that might make a good feature article?

Do you have friends or relatives who were around during the war? What were they doing? Do they have some insightful memories that could be the basis of a magazine article?

Write down some ideas on these topics and think about which publications might be interested in running the stories.

Chapter 12
Writing for the local and regional press

You might think that the local and regional press would be relatively easy to break into, but in my experience they're not and I've heard the same from other freelance writers, one of whom suggested that the editors of her local papers were so full of their own importance, that they considered freelancers to be too lowly for their paper! Fortunately, mine's not that bad! One of my earliest regular pieces of work was a slot in the 'villages' section of my local rag, writing about upcoming events. When I spoke to the editor about doing other work for them, he said he needed qualified writers with journalism degrees and an appreciation of the law - not feature writers.

Now I have wondered from time to time, if I should have borrowed a small fortune in my youth, to move away to study the course I really wanted: journalism. But in all honestly, having the wrong degrees isn't a major setback and being qualified in another topic can give you a specialism that's valuable to other publications. Also, since having that conversation with the editor of my local paper, I've sold him a reprint of a story that was published in a national magazine anyway, without any comment about my journalism qualifications. When the story's right, he's interested.

It's worth saying too, that I do own a book on journalism law, which is something worth familiarizing yourself with when you're working in this industry. Generally however, editors are much more interested in your interview contacts, the quality of your writing, the wow-factor of your photographs, and your ability to deliver good stories. No-one else has ever shown any interest in what I studied at college. I'm not going for a staff job after all. I'd much rather work as a freelance writer on my own terms.

Other regional press can be more receptive to freelancers than the local rag. The Archant group of publications include Cotswold Life, Yorkshire Life, Sussex Life and Lancashire Life, and these are just a few of the many regional magazines across the UK, published by a range of different companies. Some editors on these publications are responsive to a new angle on a regional topic, and it can be worthwhile getting to know the editors of the regional magazines where you live, because you're more likely to have stories for them, than for 'Outer Mongolia Life' - unless you live in Outer Mongolia of course!

One of my associates, Sandra Smith, writes regularly for Hertfordshire Life. She also writes artists' profiles every month for Hampshire Life, and writes monthly blog posts for both of these publications. She's a regular contributor to Buckinghamshire and Berkshire Life, submitting features on a wide range of local topics, and she has three columns in the neighbourhood news section of the local newspaper. The regional press form the bulk of her work and it's interesting to see how she works. Doing the blogs led to working for the magazines, so starting small can help you build relationships with editors that lead to greater successes.

I've sold lots of articles to regional magazines, including stories on a wildlife sanctuary to Cornwall Life and a story on a war-time nurse to Sussex Life. Holidays and people I've met have provided inspiration for these stories, because neither Cornwall, nor Sussex are my home counties. In fact my own regional publisher seems to be somewhat unresponsive to my plentiful ideas - although Sandra (above) has cracked them! I'm still working on it!

It's worth knowing that once you've cracked these markets you might receive assignments to cover other local events. At one recent press event I was invited to, the opening of a stately home for Christmas, I met freelance writers working for Buckinghamshire and Berkshire Life, the Oxford Times, and other regional publications. They had been sent to cover the story by their editors. I was there for the inspiration it might provide for a feature in the national or international press, in the months ahead.

Exercise

Think about local or regional stories that you could cover. Did you discover something really unusual on your holiday? Or is there a local artist in your home town who is doing something particularly interesting? Think about people and places that might appeal to the regional press and put out feelers for interviews with key people.

Chapter 13
Writing for religious publications

If you have a faith, or an affiliation with a religious community, you might be well placed to write articles for some of the many religious publications available today. I've had articles published in the Church of England Newspaper, Inspire Magazine, iBelieve, Direction, Good News, Woman Alive, and the Catholic Times.

Other Christian titles include the Church Times, Christianity, The Door, Liberti, and Sorted. In the USA, there are many more Christian titles and it's worth familiarising yourself with the markets in your home country if you're interested in these areas.

When you're writing for Christian magazines, it helps enormously to have church connections, whether you're a regular worshipper or not, because you'll need to call on people for interviews and statements on a wide range of topics.

Church publications are interested in real world topics including stress management, anger management, lifestyle issues, child-rearing, and relationships, as well as churchy things like how to grow the church membership, inspire from the pulpit, or lead youth group activities.

I've done interview pieces with inspirational Christians, covered church outreach initiatives and projects, and even written about health for Christian publications.

Of course there are other religious titles too:
- Muslim magazines include Emel, Sisters Magazine, and Islamique magazine.
- Pagan magazines include Pentagle, Pagan Dawn, and Witches and Pagans.
- Jewish magazines include Tablet, Moment, Jewish Living and Jewish Woman.
- The leading British atheist magazine is The New Humanist. I sold a comical article on druid ceremonies to them once.

Every religion has its own magazines. Browse the titles that interest you and see what kinds of topics they're publishing. Perhaps there's something going on at your local church that would interest them, or perhaps you have a great human interest story, which is right up their street.

There are certain etiquettes when writing for the Christian market. For example, God is always spelt with a capital G. When you refer to Him (as in God) it is always spelt with a capital H, and Lord is always spelt with a capital L.

Many of the Christian titles like to have biblical quotes included in the text to support the moral of the story, and having church leaders willing to give you a quote on a topic is always a bonus that helps add credibility to the position taken in your feature.

The stories of individuals overcoming life challenges and adversity usually end with a successful outcome that can be attributed to the goodness of God.

Popular topics include the power of prayer, innovative approaches to evangelism, Christianity at work in the third world, youth initiatives, and first person inspirational tales of happiness and success through an unwavering faith in God.

Exercise

Think about your own religious beliefs and any connections that you have with suitable interviewees for religious publications. What's new in your local church, mosque or synagogue? What's inspiring for other people to read about?

Jot down some ideas and think about which publications might be interested in your stories.

Chapter 14
Writing travel articles

Perhaps one of the most desirable areas of freelance writing is travel writing. Travel publications include High Life - the British Airways magazine, Coast, National Geographic, Britain, and Wanderlust.

Many airlines have in-flight magazines that offer opportunities for freelancers and you don't need to travel abroad to contribute. An article about your home town might appeal to readers who are visiting the UK from overseas.

I've written hundreds of travel articles covering different aspects of the UK including parts of Scotland, the south coast, Wales, London, and my home county of Buckinghamshire.

Think about interesting places you've visited and which magazines might be interested in an article on those locations. Don't feel limited to the travel press either. Women's magazines, nostalgic publications, the local press, and specialist publications all run travel features. Opportunities abound in this sector.

Try to think about interesting angles on travel destinations. I've written about Victorian workhouses that are open to the public, stately homes, and events coming up across the UK. There are few limits to the opportunities here, but the challenge might be finding a new angle that hasn't been covered a million times before.

Some travel writers cover local food and restaurants. This can be particularly interesting if the destination is overseas and the local delicacy is insects or ostrich meat.

Many magazines love to hear about exotic locations. One thing that's really important for any travel article is the availability of excellent, high resolution photographs. The standard of photography in this sector is very high and it's worth investing in some decent photography equipment and getting some training if you aspire to do more work in this sector. I find it very rewarding, so I think it's worth the investment.

Think about overseas travel that you've experienced or have planned. Have you been to the Grand Canyon, the Taj Mahal, or seen the Leaning Tower of Pisa? Have you experienced the culture shock of a break in rural Africa, or do you have an interesting perspective on the theme parks of Orlando?

Each of these travel topics could have appeal to a wide range of magazines. Bring the experience to life with your words and pictures, draw the reader in to your journey and make them wish they were there.

If readers are really inspired by your article, they might write to the publications' letters page saying they've booked a holiday there themselves. That's happened to me a few times. It feels good. It authenticates your skill as a travel writer and assures you that you've written an inspiring story that the readers enjoyed.

Exercise
Have you been on an African safari and taken great photos? Have you been to Iceland and got amazing pictures of the geysers, volcanoes and waterfalls? Who wouldn't be interested in that!

If you've been to some amazing places and got great photos of the experience, work up some compelling angles for a feature article, and pitch your idea to the editor of a travel magazine. It might pay for your holiday.

Chapter 15
Writing for children

Writing for children requires attention to your vocabulary and the words that modern children use. Language is very age-specific, and when you're writing for the young end of the market, you'll need to use simple words, not teen slang - and vice versa. Most children's magazines have specific styles, and you need to match them to succeed in these markets.

Children's magazines include Girl Talk, Okido, Eco Kids, Story Time, RSPCA Animal Action, and National Geographic Kids.

I've written for a children's animal magazines about a wide variety of wild animals, and I've also done a fair bit of work for kiddies' general interest publications. I've covered everything from abandoned bunnies at rescue centres, to Hans Christian Andersen, painting giraffes, breeds of guinea pig, and pathogenic fungi.

Kids' magazines are open to all sorts of fascinating topics. They're not particularly easy to break into, but once you're known, they can provide repeat business.

Like adult publications, each children's magazine has its own areas of interest - some are niche and others are general. There's a publication called First News that explains the news in a way that children can understand. There are also girls magazines focused on crafts; teen magazines focused on boy bands, relationships and fashion; and special interest magazines for all age groups. You need to hone and polish your story for a suitable publication, just as you do for the adult markets.

Morals
When you're writing fiction for children, many people like to include a moral undertone: the good guy wins for example, and being unkind doesn't pay. Recent research shows that, "a moral story that praises a character's honesty is more effective at getting young children to tell the truth than a story that emphasizes the negative repercussions of lying. The findings suggest that stories such as 'The Boy Who Cried Wolf' and 'Pinocchio' may not be the best cautionary tales when it comes to inspiring honest behaviour in children."
www.sciencedaily.com/releases /2014/12/141208144150.htm

If moral behaviour in children is one of your goals while writing for this market, it seems to make sense therefore, to tell tales about an honest person being rewarded, rather than a bad guy being punished.

Inspiration

Michael Morpurgo is the author of the best-selling children's book War Horse, which has been made into a Hollywood movie. He started his career as a primary school teacher, and developed a fascination with the First World War.

At a literary festival in 2014 he told a hall full of children, "I was inspired to write War Horse by a man who told me that his best friend during WWI was his horse. It might sound a bit sentimental but this wasn't a silly, sentimental man. He was a tough soldier, who had been through the worst of times. He said he could talk to his horse when no-one else would listen, and depend on the horse during times of conflict. Approximately the same number of horses died in WWI as people, and it was research into this kind of history that inspired me to delve deeper and write the story of War Horse."

When a child at the festival asked him, "What makes you write about sad things?" he replied, "Life is a mixture of sad times and happy times. People die, animals die, and bad things happen. My writing reflects the realities of life – the good things and the bad. I don't write just for the reader. I write about the things that interest me, and sometimes these things are sad."

Exercise

Get copies of some of the children's magazines that you'd like to write for. What are they publishing? What do the kids you know enjoy reading? Think through some suitable topics and write down some ideas for stories you could offer to children's publications.

Chapter 16
Writing for specialist and trade publications

My 15 year career in corporate and educational marketing gave me experience working in consultancies, in educational institutions, and in trade associations. During this time, I developed enough insight about some of these industries to appreciate the issues they were facing and to write articles on topics relevant to some of these industries.

I was familiar with military resettlement publications from my years in university marketing roles. So I wrote about how to get into marketing for a military resettlement magazine. I'd been through the whole caboodle of professional marketing qualifications, so was well placed to write about the process. I'd studied right up to master's degree level part-time, while working my way up the organisational hierarchy. This gave me the insight to write about the qualifications required, topics covered, and dedication required to pass the exams.

I also covered the diverse opportunities open to people once you get into marketing, and the scope for specialising in different areas of expertise, such as digital media, customer relationship management, advertising, or public relations.

I also sold articles to Leader magazine - a title published by the Association of Schools and Colleges, because I had insight into some of the challenges faced by people working in academia. I sold them articles about stress management, healthy eating, and social media.

I had a four year spell working for a technology consultancy and my professional background gave me the insight to write stories on business topics for a wide variety of related publications including IT Europa and other niche business titles.

Think back to your work and business experience. What expertise can you draw on for your writing career? If you have experience in teaching, then there are plenty of teaching magazines looking for new angles on topical subjects. All industries have their own magazines and whether your background is woodworking, horticulture, nursing, veterinary care, secretarial work or engineering, there's a trade publication out there, that targets your industry. All you need to do is work out what areas are topical that you could cover for them.

Exercise

Think about your contacts - is there anyone who would make a good interviewee? Think widely about topics and angles that you can offer the trade press in your specialist industry. Show your expertise, make the most of your contacts, and they shouldn't be too difficult to break into if you present the right story idea and sell yourself as an expert willing to write the piece.

Chapter 17
Writing for overseas markets

Some of my most regular clients are US magazines. In fact, I find it easier to get commissions from publications in the USA than from the local and regional press in my home county of Buckinghamshire! I also do some work for Australian magazines.

As a British writer, I'm sometimes able to offer overseas publications something a bit different from their regular writers. They'll call on me to cover British events, or write about British topics or locations. They're also open to nutrition articles - health and obesity are big issues in America.

Likewise, I imagine if you're an overseas writer touting to British publications, you'll be able to offer something quite different to what we Brits are able to provide. Sometimes this can work in your favour.

There are obviously language differences to consider. These are particularly prevalent when you're talking about foods. In America, an aubergine is called an egg plant. A courgette is called a zucchini, and they have a shortage of 'u's - by that I mean, they spell colour, color; honour, honor; favour, favor; and labour, labor. Americans have centers, not centres. They have theaters, not theatres. They go to 'school' even in their late teens - a term used to describe colleges or universities. They write you - they don't write 'to' you. They have flashlights, not torches. The list goes on.

It helps to familiarise yourself with these Americanisms, so that you can try to get your work for those markets as accurate as possible. Do it well, and they'll want to use you again. Do it badly, and they might steer clear of you in the future.

There are differences in punctuation too. In the US, when you're writing dialogue, it's correct to close quotations with punctuation inside the quote marks. In the UK, it depends on whether the punctuation relates to the quoted words or the whole sentence. That said, we are adopting more Americanisms here in the UK, so it might ultimately come down to what it says in a publication's style guide.

Styles do vary between publications. My local newspaper has adopted the Economist's style guide, along with American date formatting and other things that just feel wrong in the UK!

Punctuation conventions aren't as critical as getting the language right, or simply paying attention to the style guide. Americans sometimes like to use two dashes -- like this, rather than one - like this. Again, that's more of a style preference, which varies between publications. Chicken Soup for the Soul has a style guide in which they ask authors to use two dashes not one. It looks odd to me, but I'm British! Most publications have subeditors who'll sort out these discrepancies if you don't get it quite right. They don't all issue style guides, so if in doubt, check a previous issue of the publication to see what convention they use.

Payment

When you work for overseas publications, you get paid in their currency. There are a few options for cashing foreign cheques in the UK. At the time of writing, the big clearing banks, such as Lloyds, Halifax, and TSB will charge you about £8 for the transaction plus whatever their conversion rate to sterling is at the time - it's worth checking their fees before you pay it in if this is important to you. The smaller institutions, like Nationwide Building Society may have higher rates for changing foreign cheques to sterling. When you go to pay in a foreign cheque, you'll be presented with a detailed form and the clerk will help you fill it out if you're stuck. You get used to it when you do a lot of work overseas.

The alternative is to open a bank account in the foreign currency for which you are working. This avoids paying so many transaction fees and might be worth considering if you do a lot of work for publications in a foreign country, but there are fees for these accounts so it may not be worthwhile. Ask your bank about the options available if this interests you.

Getting money changed might seem like a lot of hassle, but it isn't really. The major bonus I find about writing for the US markets is that they are totally clear about the terms they are offering. They will usually know exactly when they are going to print your article. They will state up front how much they will pay, and will ask you to sign a contract to that effect. They usually pay promptly, and in my experience they don't hold articles for years. I have never had a US editor change their mind. They seem to give a much greater degree of commitment to a writer when they commission work, than some editors do in the UK. This is reflected in the contract - the commitment works on both sides.

As a new writer for an American publication, you'll probably be sent a US tax declaration form - fill it out and return it to declare that you are living outside the USA and you don't have to pay US taxes. Obviously you declare the income on your British tax return when it's due.

The US publications do have some tough contract terms that you have to sign if you wish to work for them. You have to accept all responsibility if someone sues them over something relating to your article. This feels uncomfortable and is a good reason to be dead sure that your work isn't going to offend anyone! On the upside, these contracts usually contain a kill fee, payable in the event of them changing their minds. It's a step up from British publications, some of whom expect you to accept 100% of the fallout - eg. nothing for all your hard work - if they change their minds.

In some cases, your interviewees will also be asked to sign forms declaring that they accept responsibility if anyone sues the magazine because of your article. This too, feels very uncomfortable when you ask your interviewee to sign something saying they accept responsibility if your article results in legal action. If you work overseas a lot, it's worth considering getting writers' insurance for these eventualities, and of course, then you're covered for your work in the UK too. The only thing is, some insurers won't cover writing published outside the UK, and others ramp the price up when you mention America.

The challenges of overseas publishing also include the practicalities of trying to find out when your work is published. You have to rely upon a communicative editorial team, who will send you copies, PDFs, or as a bear minimum, let you know when it's out. However, these details are often stated in the contract, so at least you have some idea what to expect.

I did have one Australian health magazine who pushed back my article to a summer special edition without mentioning it. This meant that publication and payment were both delayed, but at least when I queried it, the editor was quick to respond and put me in the picture.

When you sell articles overseas, you can sell First North American Rights, or First Australian Rights, without affecting your rights to sell the article in the UK, where you can still offer First British Serial Rights. This means each publication gets to print it first in their own country. Most publications have an aversion to reprints, and many publications won't accept reprints of articles that have already appeared in their home country, but they're less likely to mind if it's been printed elsewhere in the world, but not on their home turf.

Publishers often say they'd like World Rights because they want the option to put it on their websites too. I've occasionally had to explain to a US publisher that a similar piece has already been published in the UK, but they're welcome to have First North American print rights, and to use it on their website. They're usually OK about that.

Working for overseas publications is an interesting experience, with some drawbacks, but on balance, I'd recommend it.

American magazines and newspapers are listed in Writers' Market - the US equivalent of the Writers' and Artists' Yearbook here in the UK. Australian magazines and newspapers are listed in The Australian Writers' Marketplace, an online membership facility that is the Aussie equivalent.

You can also find foreign publications simply by searching online. It's a good idea to check out foreign magazine's websites before pitching, because the sites give you a feel for what they publish and may contain writers' guidelines.

There are many wonderful opportunities around the globe for determined writers wanting to break into new markets. Magazines written in English are also published in India and many other parts of the world. Look beyond the obvious English-speaking countries to any culture with which you have an affinity, and explore the opportunities for written works.

Chapter 18
Writing interview pieces

I've recently interviewed a Butlin's redcoat, a beekeeper, and a group of women with embarrassing problems! Being comfortable with interviewing people can be an important part of being a successful freelance writer.

Interview assignments can take you out and about meeting new people, seeing new things, and enjoying new experiences. I've had hundreds of interview pieces published and met all sorts of interesting people in the process, covering everything from military history to dancing dogs, to blind bowling and a stamp-collecting fish-keeper. I've even interviewed a woman who, with friends, carries a ten foot wooden cross 12 miles through the countryside every Easter, to a holy shrine in Walsingham.

We live in a fascinating world of interesting and eccentric characters, just waiting to be discovered by those with an eye for a story and a determined approach to getting published.

Last year I interviewed six writers for my first book, 'Freelance Writing on Health, Food and Gardens', to get six different perspectives on their writing roles in these three specialist areas. It was one of the most enjoyable elements of writing the book and it showed the diversity and scope of these topics, which on the face of it appear niche, but really, they're not as specialist as they might seem. They're huge topics with massive potential for aspiring writers! One interviewee was mainly a travel writer doing restaurant reviews as he travelled, and another was a garden designer with a regular column in BBC Gardener's World magazine. I find it fascinating to hear how other freelancers get on working in this industry, and hear about their triumphs and mishaps along the way. I can relate to many of their stories!

As a writer, I find interview pieces one of the easiest and most rewarding assignments. However, some people find conducting interviews quite difficult, so here are some pointers to help you get the most from your interview opportunities.

Who to approach first

The question I'm most frequently asked about interviews, is whether to approach the interviewee or the editor first.

You need to be confident that you can get the interview *before* approaching an editor with your idea, so it's always advisable to run your idea past your proposed interviewee first, and get their agreement in principle.

Yes, it can be disappointing if you have an interviewee psyched up and ready to go, and then you can't seem to sell the story. That's happened to me a few times! However it's even worse to get a sale on a story and then have to confess that you can't deliver it, because your proposed interviewee won't play ball!

I made that mistake once. I assumed that a lady who'd willingly done an interview about her dancing dog would be willing to do an interview about her 10 bouncing bunnies, but when I contacted her after securing a commission for the piece, she said one of them had just died, and she didn't feel able to do the interview because she was so upset. She then moved and everything got complicated. The assignment collapsed. Fortunately, the editor forgave me!

Another problem with interviews is if its a celebrity, or someone who you're not sure will respond to your request. The most likely people to help you are those people trying to promote something. My recent interview with a Butlin's redcoat was part of a book promotion, featuring a series of redcoats from the 1960s. Her publisher was more than willing to set up the interview and send me some photos.

Preparing questions

It's always a good idea to prepare a list of open-ended questions in advance. This will focus your mind on what you want to know, and ensure you don't forget anything critical before the conclusion of the interview. It's obviously better to get everything in one hit than have to go back and ask more questions later!

Your prepared questions will be a valuable prompt, but if the interviewee veers off track, just keep listening and evaluate what they're saying. Interviewees often have valuable insights on related topics that you may not have considered. If their diversion is relevant to your article – or would make useful information for another feature – let them continue. It could improve your interview piece, or provide valuable material for another project.

Sometimes however, these diversions are not relevant, nor are they particularly interesting. When this happens, just take the lead and gently steer your interviewee back onto topic.

If your interviewee's answers are a bit short, don't be afraid to ask them to elaborate. Dig deeper, be curious, and try to anticipate what your editor and readers will want to know. Take detailed notes or use a Dictaphone to record the conversation, with the interviewee's permission.

Face-to-face interviews

Where possible, it's best to conduct interviews face to face because you're better able to develop a rapport with your interviewee and pick up on all the non-verbal cues that don't come across over the phone or by email. Often the interview environment, the interviewee's mannerisms, their dress-sense, and the environment, can add interest to your article and help bring the interview piece to life. It provides an opportunity to get photographs for your article too.

Depending on the topic, they might be able to give you demonstrations of their work, or show you things they've collected, which you wouldn't otherwise see or experience.

Telephone and email

Telephone or email interviews can work when it's not practical to meet in person. Telephone still enables you to pick up on some cues, and to have a more fluid conversation that might bring out unexpected responses. Email is great if your interviewee doesn't like being put on the spot and prefers to prepare their answers carefully in their own time.

Double Checking

Some writers are very reluctant to show an interviewee the final article, but I think it's important to have flexibility on this matter. If you're writing about technical issues, health issues, or someone with a sensitive story to tell, it makes sense to get things approved. You want to be sure that the technical details are accurate, the health advice is properly conveyed, and that the sensitive story is told in such a way that your interviewee is happy with it. On contentious topics, it's also possible that misquotes could result in legal action, so you want to be sure that you've got everything down accurately.

Some interviewees have complete faith in me and aren't worried at all about seeing the final copy. That's fine, but if the interviewee is nervous or the topic is technical or sensitive, I always get my final copy approved. Sometimes they have second thoughts about revealing information, and other times, they'd just like something phrased differently.

My tendency to check the final copy with interviewees did go wrong once – it was an interview piece with a gardener at a stately home. Upon final approval, he completely rewrote it and took out all the quotes. It was completely unusable. I did manage to salvage the situation, by getting the PR team involved. The piece was rescued two days before deadline!

For this reason, I don't offer copy for final approval unless I feel it's really necessary, but there is a balance to be struck, and I'm pleased to report that in over four years of professional freelance writing, that approach has only gone wrong once. I keep my interviewees happy and they're usually happy to be interviewed again for another article. That's a valuable resource to have on hand.

Chapter 19
Inspiration

"How do you come up with ideas?"

It's a question I'm often asked and the answer is easy, because ideas are all around me. The skill is in being able to recognise good stories and place them with suitable publications - that comes with practice.

While showing some of my published work to members of my local writers' group recently, I was asked how I came up with the idea for a piece about dancing dogs. I told them that I volunteer for the local branch of the RSPCA and at their annual social event, there was a performing dog doing tricks. It sparked an idea to write on the topic for Dogs Monthly, and a number of interviews with the trainer ensued. I wrote more articles on similar themes for other publications.

Think widely about article topics as you go about your daily life and you'll find fascinating subjects all around you.

Email alerts
I have email alerts delivered by 'Science Daily' because they provide hooks and inspiration for feature ideas. It keeps me up to date with recent research in the fields of health and nutrition, and fills me in on other research projects that might be useful or interesting.

Foodie topics
In my role as a health and food writer, I've written on all sorts of varied topics, covering healthy eating and recipes. I've also written about visiting breweries and covered stories about vineyards on the south coast.

There are many opportunities to write about foodie topics. You could interview the owner of a thriving cake-making business, do restaurant reviews, or cover the gourmet delicacies of rural Africa.

Holidays
Holidays are a lovely way to get inspiration for articles about historic locations, travel, and different cultures. You might meet some interesting people on holiday too. I once stayed in a holiday

apartment where the owner had left her high flying job in London to move south and renovate a derelict building into self contained flats. She let the apartments out to holidaymakers and the venture enabled her to enjoy a more idyllic life in the Devon countryside. There are stories everywhere you go. It's just a matter of being tuned in to stories that might be of interest to the press whether local, regional, national or overseas.

Local events

I went to see a musician play at a local church recently and, during a break in the performance, the pastor gave a short talk about their evangelical work. The church had used a caravan to engage with troubled teenagers on the streets. That short presentation triggered an idea for a Christian publication. I set up an interview with the pastor about their youth work, and sold the story to Inspire magazine.

Pets

My pet guinea pigs have inspired many stories for specialist and children's magazines, as well as appearing on the pets pages of true life magazines for £25 a pop - before the budgets were slashed! Every aspect of their lives ends up in a magazine, from adoption, to veterinary visits, to food preferences and insurance. One day, one of the guinea pigs became ill and the vet said he was allergic to his bedding. So I pitched to a number of pet magazines offering to research the concept of guinea pigs being allergic to their bedding!

Flicking through magazines

In the summer, when I need inspiration, I sit in the garden with a pile of magazines and try to generate my own ideas based on some of the topics they've covered recently. Even old copies can be useful. I had a copy of Prima that inspired a wealth of Christmas ideas one year, when I'd been struggling for Christmas inspiration. Even the readers' letters provide topics for feature articles.

Neighbourhood disputes

Perhaps one of the most classic sources of inspiration was a neighbourhood dispute last year. I was so annoyed that I decided to write about it! The problem was that we bought a small van and one of our neighbours didn't like it. The chap two doors down keeps a canal boat on his front lawn, so we never considered that a little van would get tempers flaring. Our neighbour told us to put it into storage. He never wanted to see it again.

Being a writer, at home all day, I found falling out with the neighbours quite upsetting - especially when they gave me disapproving looks through the window. I wrote an article about our neighbourhood dispute to a consumer title.

Stately homes

I live close to one of the National Trust's most beautiful properties, Waddesdon Manor, and this year I was invited to the press launch of their Lights and Legends Christmas display. Bruce Munro, the famous light artist, was present to tell us about the inspiration for his latest creation. As dusk turned to night, he took us on a walk through the grounds to see the installations in all their glory. It's well worth a visit if you happen to be in Buckinghamshire one December, as it happens every year!

By December, it's way too late for me to generate any Christmas commissions from this visit - I don't work for the dailies. Most of my customers are thinking about next June by December! But it wouldn't surprise me if the visit to Waddesdon Manor provides inspiration for another article in the summertime, when my clients are thinking about Christmas again!

Literary festivals

My links to the local photographic society led to work at Thame Arts and Literary Festival. I've been a member of the Photographic Society for two years now, and the Festival organisers were desperately seeking a photographer for the event, days before it was due to start. I put myself forward and became the official photographer.

As a bonus, I had free entry into all the events where I could hear the author's talks, and find inspiration for articles. I attended BBC Radio 4's Any Questions and got some great photos of Michael Heseltine and Jonathan Dimbleby. It was certainly a very varied and interesting festival, with a topical focus on WWI. Among the better-known authors speaking, was the author of War Horse, Michael

Morpurgo. I later pitched an idea to a writing magazine, to cover his talk - something I could do because I'd taken notes and had good pictures of him, using a telephoto lens from the back of the room.

These kinds of events can be useful for inspiration. The Thame Arts and Literary Festival had writing workshops, film events, a Midsummer Murders Walk, speakers, music, a comedian, and a wide variety of authors present. I later wrote about the festival in a travel magazine.

As you can see, there is inspiration all around you - from social events and email alerts, to neighbourhood disputes. Keep your eyes peeled and take notes on everything. You never know when they might come in handy!

Chapter 20
Learning from rejection

When I started freelance writing for a living in 2011, my dad (always the optimist) said I wouldn't succeed. It was too competitive in his opinion.

I ignored him and did my best to break into the market because it's all I've ever wanted to do. I proved him wrong, and proved to myself that I could make a success of my dream - because when I started, I didn't know if it was going to succeed or not!

To give dad due credit, since then he's appeared in a couple of my articles and seems to be moderately enthusiastic about my writing career now. Sometimes you just need to be thick skinned and get on with it. I'll admit to being about as thick skinned as a skeleton sometimes, but on this occasion I was hugely driven anyway and his opinion came as no great surprise. He's always favoured steady, 'proper' jobs over anything too ambitious.

However, even when your friends and family are on your side, freelance writing can be a perilous occupation. You may feel bombarded by rejection letters! Don't let this get you down. Think of rejection letters as opportunities, not set-backs. If I get a rejection letter I'm pleased because it means the editor thinks enough of my pitch to make the effort to communicate with me about it. That's a great start! Perhaps next time, my idea will fit his or her editorial requirements better!

As time passes, my hit rate is increasing, and I spend much more time writing than pitching. When I started writing for a living it was very definitely the other way around! Writing is a profession riddled with rejection, but there are ways of turning it around and turning rejections into sales. These are some of my experiences...

Lesson 1: Forget the glossy magazines and concentrate on the niche titles

For years when I was younger, trying to break into freelance writing I was pitching to the big titles - the ones I could borrow from the library because they were free and I was broke. But they were mostly glossy magazines that are really difficult to break into. At the time, I didn't realise the error of my approach.

Since relaunching myself as a writer and doing it more successfully, I've realised that targeting niche titles is a much more successful approach. If you know about railways, there are dozens of railway magazines looking at everything from heritage railways to the latest news in the railway industry.

If you're an expert on a certain sport, then the sporting titles might be interested to hear from you. I know a cricket coach who is a freelance writer and he works for many of the major cricket titles, with the added bonus that the publisher sets up interviews for him with professional players.

The lesson learnt
Some people do get an early break with the likes of Cosmopolitan, Marie Claire, or Good Housekeeping, but they are few and far between. Most of us are more likely to succeed if we target niche titles that fit with our areas of expertise.

Lesson 2: Be self-critical and think laterally
A few years ago, I pitched an idea to cover Benjamin Disraeli's life to a literary publication. He'd been a successful writer in his day as well as a politician in the late 19th century. The editor was more interested in his literary works than his biography, so she invited me to speculatively submit a piece on Benjamin Disraeli's first novel, Vivian Grey, instead. I hadn't read the book, but as it turned out, it was a reflection of his life, so it wasn't too far off my original idea anyway. It was "the memoirs he never wrote" said one critic.

I accepted the challenge and headed off to Disraeli's former home, Hughenden Manor in Buckinghamshire, to research the former Prime Minister and his literary works. A guided tour brought Disraeli's home to life, but when I tried to read the book, I found it so old fashioned, it was hard to understand. I skipped a few chapters, and read reviews to get a feel for what the experts thought.

The whole experience was a true education - I returned from Hughenden Manor with a much better appreciation of how Disraeli's literary works reflected his life experiences. But in my enthusiasm, I submitted the article prematurely, and it was rejected on the grounds that it needed livening up. It was a bit dry.

I put it aside for a few weeks and then took a fresh look at it. After a break, I could see the problem – it lacked a modern spark. So I brought Harry Potter into the story and likened the aspersions made in Vivian Grey to modern-day scandals.

When I resubmitted it a couple of weeks later, the response that came back was wonderful. The editor said it was much improved and accepted it for publication. I'd transformed this historic story into a modern upbeat piece on high society scandals. In truth, the hard work had already been completed. It just needed a fresh look and a sprinkle of imagination to bring it to life!

The lesson learnt

Take a step back from your work and look at it critically. Is it too dry? Is it the wrong style? It may help to take a break for a week or two and come back to it.

Lesson 3: Follow up whatever opportunities are available

I came back from South Wales, completely inspired by a wonderful walk we had done on our holiday, and pitched it to Country Walking magazine. It had everything: fascinating geology, fossils to find and enjoy, and colourful rocks that took my breath away - but Jenny, the editor, said they weren't commissioning new writers and had enough feature material for the year ahead.

She did however, point me to their Walking Routes section, saying that whilst submissions were not guaranteed to be printed, they were happy to accept items from new writers in that section. I've since sold them lots of walking routes with more in the pipeline. The first was the walk along the South Wales coast with photographs of the fossils we found. The second was a walk through the Buckinghamshire hills to a haunted cave. My most recent submission to them was a stroll around Hughenden Manor's wider estate - it's interesting how one story leads to another isn't it!

The lesson learnt

Think beyond your initial idea to embrace other opportunities that come up. Just because a publication is full up with features, it doesn't mean there are no opportunities. See if you can engage with the editor to find out what freelance opportunities are available, however small.

Lesson 4: Great writers were rejected too

It's always comforting to be reminded that even the most respected writers have suffered rejection. On a recent visit to Beatrice Potter's Lake District home, Hill Top, I saw a letter from Country Life magazine rejecting three of her stories whilst accepting the fourth. It served as another reminder that even those whose brilliance has inspired generations, get rejected in their early years.

Reading Beatrice Potter's rejection letter from Country Life reminded me of the last conversation I had with them: I'd pitched an idea by email to write about Castle Drogo and another, as a qualified nutritionist, to write about the healing power of home grown vegetables. They telephoned me to say they intended to cover Castle Drogo but they wanted an architectural expert to do it. I wasn't the right person for the job.

I asked about the garden vegetable nutrition idea and they said: "Why would we want you to write our gardening features when we have Alan Titchmarch?" The answer was easy - I'm a qualified nutritionist offering to provide a nutrition angle on vegetable gardening - something Alan Titchmarsh simply isn't qualified to do. I was passed onto the gardening editor, but it was too peripheral to their gardening theme.

The lesson learnt

You can't win them all! I'd pitched a topic they wanted to cover, but they didn't feel I had the expertise for the job. Focus on titles and topics where you can deliver the expertise required and you'll have a greater chance of success.

Lesson 5: When the editor is giving you feedback, listen and learn!

When I wrote to the editor of Good Motoring offering to cover the experience of being a learner motorcyclist, he rejected the idea, but I was invited to submit ideas related to road safety instead. I was delighted to be given the opportunity and secured a commission to write about how good nutrition can help you concentrate on the road, followed by one about the results of speed camera studies.

The lesson learnt

These little gems in rejection letters, open up an opportunity to pitch an idea that the editors want to buy. Look for small gems of information and occasionally you'll find an opportunity right up your street.

Lesson 6: The appeal of good photographs

Over the years I've pitched to women's magazines and gardening magazines hundreds of times and sometimes the story is great, but the thing that prevents me from getting the commission is the photographs. This was much more of a problem in my early years than it is today, because in recent years I've been on a photography course, invested in a decent camera, and done what it takes to take my writing and photographic services to the next level.

For those people interested in targeting image-led magazines with their writing, or even those who just want to improve their photography for publication, it's well worth investing in training and equipment.

After much agonising over which camera to buy, looking at different reviews of entry-level DSLRs, I bought a Nikon 3100. Initially I was disappointed by the results, but as I learnt to use it properly, and invested in digital enhancement software, my photos improved dramatically.

In an introductory photography course, you'll look at using apertures, shutter speeds, white balance, and when it's beneficial to overexpose and underexpose your pictures. If you choose an introductory course, you'll probably learn the best settings and techniques for sport, landscapes and for portrait photography. You'll get feedback on your photographs and learn more about how to get the best from your camera, whether you're using a compact or an expensive piece of kit. Just remember that for some publications, the images are just as important as the words.

The lesson learnt

You can take your writing to the next level by providing stunning photographs to accompany your work. Take a look at the magazines you're targeting and the chances are, they're running excellent photos alongside the articles. If you can provide photos of the same standard, you stand a much greater chance of having work accepted.

Chapter 21
Checking your work

A crucially important part of the successful writer's skillset, is the ability to accumulate correct and current information. The internet is abundant with out of date and incorrect information. It's all too easy to take 'facts' that you find on websites as gospel, only to discover, too late, that they've got their information wrong.

Don't believe what you read until you've double checked

When you're researching stories for articles, don't rely on the accuracy of one source. Just a few days ago, I was writing about Montacute House for a US magazine. The guidebook - a rather old one - said the House's construction began in 1588. Wikipedia said the House's construction began in about 1598. An official document on the National Trust's website (they own the estate) said construction began in the 1590s, and English Heritage said building began in 1598-99.

While I would ordinarily expect the guide book to be correct, this is not the first time I've encountered inaccuracies in National Trust literature - nor on Wikipedia for that matter! The balance of opinion seemed to point to the 1590s and the National Trust's position had changed since the guide book was published. I suspect the truth is that no-one's too sure exactly when construction started. However, further investigation revealed that in 1588 Sir Edward Phelips inherited the land on which Montacute was later built, but he didn't actually start construction of the property for another decade, so the guidebook was wrong and the website was correct. It's just as well that I double checked!

Wikipedia

Some years ago, I had a short spell working for the Chartered Institute of Marketing (CIM), during which time, I was tasked with getting the CIM Wikipedia description accurate. *Simple!* I thought, and proceeded to amend all the inaccuracies on the Wikipedia page online. I announced when I'd done it and patted myself on the back.

24 hours later, all my amendments had been deleted - disapproved by the authorities in Wikipedia. They said that the

information about the Institute had to be referenced from a third party website, not from the Institute itself. I was amazed. As the only definitive source of accurate information about the CIM, is the Institute itself, I was at a loss to understand why we had to find an alternative site to provide accurate details of the membership terms and benefits.

It was obvious that the information on Wikipedia was wrong, but I was forced to enter into a frustrated debate about it on their user forum and they wouldn't budge. Wikipedia threatened to delete the whole article if I didn't stop trying to correct it, and as my superiors felt it was better to have wrong information there, than no information at all, I was eventually forced to give up.

The message for writers? Take care over what you believe when you're using the internet as a reference source for your articles. Check on the definitive guide for the subject area, as some sites carry information that is incorrect, and getting it changed can be extremely difficult.

Preparing events calendars
On a similar note, when you're asked to prepare an article about events coming up in six months time for a magazine that likes to work well ahead of schedule, be warned that many events organisers don't update their websites until a few months before the event. Some of them don't even decide what they're doing until a few months before, which can make life tricky. The key is to identify those annual events where the date is set for the following year as soon as the previous year's event has finished.

It's easy to make a mistake if organisers don't put the year on their website. I made the mistake once of listing a November fireworks event on the wrong date because the organisers had not updated their website from the previous year when I was writing the article in September. There was no year given on the website, and I stupidly assumed that the details advertised were for the forthcoming event in two months time, not for the previous year's celebrations. However, after it went to print, a reader got in touch with the editorial team to say they'd printed the wrong date. I checked and the website had changed in the intervening period.

They still didn't give the year, but the event was clearly on a different date. I've never made that mistake since.

Don't make assumptions about things like that. If in doubt, check and double check. It's not a good feeling to get that email from the editor, saying that a reader has pointed out that your information is wrong!

Travel information

If you get the opportunity to write up a holiday experience do check that nothing has closed since your visit. I was planning to mention a zoo that I'd visited in a travel article, but upon investigation I discovered that the zoo had closed. Yes, there were internet references suggesting the zoo was still open, but the website had shut down, the animals had been rehomed, and the zoo had become the estate of a luxury hotel. It also transpired that the council hadn't taken the road signs down so families were still turning up expecting to find a zoo. Apparently some were bitterly disappointed. It's just as well then, that the former zoo never made it into my travel article. I wouldn't want to add to the sense of disappointment around the attraction's demise.

Check web links

Web links are changing constantly, and it's worth checking the web links on your manuscript at the last minute, because they might change between production of your first draft and the final submission. When I wrote my first book, I planned to include the government's website initiative, Get British Business Online, but between me preparing the first draft and the final proof from the publishers, the government scheme and its website had closed. On something like a book you can't control what happens online after publication, but you can at least do your best to make sure it's current at the time of going to print.

Chapter 22
Getting paid

Getting paid as a freelance writer is always a precarious area. Most magazines and newspapers pay on publication and some publishers hold onto articles for years before using them, which means getting paid can take years. You need exceptional organisational skills to keep track of who's paid, and what's still outstanding. You need a solid invoicing process, and a follow up process that chases both scheduling of articles that have been outstanding for a long time, and payment of articles that have been published. A decent bank balance or a second income to pay the bills is helpful too!

The challenge of getting paid has reached a whole new level of ridiculousness since I wrote my last book in 2013. It was becoming a bit of a joke even then, but I was pretty proud of myself for having built up a full-time workload as a freelance writer during the economic recession.

In the last few years however, I've really started to feel the hit from the credit crunch, despite the apparent brightening economic outlook! Some magazines in the UK slashed their fees by 25%, while a US magazine who I work for regularly, slashed their fees by two thirds! I managed to renegotiate and get a one-third pay cut instead.

Meanwhile, I withdrew an article submission from another magazine, because of their abysmally slow payment. One of my earlier articles appeared on their website, four months after it had appeared in print (I'd missed it). I invoiced promptly, thinking they'd pay promptly. Not so.

Months of chasing, broken promises, and an eight month delay ensued. I was furious about being ignored and fobbed off. I felt convinced that I wasn't going to get paid at all. I eventually threatened them with the small claims court and got paid. It was only £120 and it took them eight months to pay. I withdrew the next article because it wasn't worth the aggravation and I've since sold it to another buyer - and been paid.

On another occasion, the editor of an entirely different publication commissioned an article for an anniversary event but didn't run it. The reason: "We have so much material!" It was difficult to place it elsewhere because of the time-sensitive nature of the article. I'd put a lot of time into it and had driven miles to take accompanying photographs but they didn't even pay a kill fee. It was very irritating, especially as it was the second time they'd done that to me in a year. They'd published, and paid for, two of my articles the previous year, but I don't like my work being treated as disposable, so I don't pitch to them any more. Incidentally, I did manage to rewrite it and place it with another publication, but then the editor changed and the decision about whether or not to use it, now hangs in the balance!

A military publication scrapped a 'readers page' that I wrote for regularly before they'd used all the commissioned articles. When I asked for a kill fee on a piece about two wrens, I was told, "We don't offer kill fees, sorry - but we will continue to commission work from you." I just hope they don't scrap the other key pages I write for, before they've used the new commissions! Fortunately, I managed to rehome half the article with a regional publication, and I'm optimistic about the other half being accepted by a different regional magazine.

A fish keeping publication that I did a lot of work for went out of print. The editor paid a 50% kill fee for three articles outstanding, and it seems they're in talks about the possibility of reviving the publication as a digital magazine, so I may yet get the other 50%! Let's hope so.

A paranormal publication that became an early casualty of the economic recession, turned to digital issues only, and stopped paying their writers due to economic constraints. They didn't pay a kill fee for the unused articles on their files and I've been unable to place the articles elsewhere. Perhaps one day I'll find them a new home... but that title was so niche, there's not much out there like it!

A regional magazine commissioned an article on a war-time story and when it still hadn't been used after two years, I started to chase. The editor said she'd still use it and explained that time-sensitive material just kept getting in first! But as the months and years passed, the editor eventually took to ignoring me. I am now looking to rehome it.

I had a particularly unpleasant experience when one editor changed recently. His predecessor had commissioned (and accepted) a series of articles for publication, but did say there would be delays in publishing them because he had a lot of backlog. He duly published something of mine about once a quarter, but not necessarily in date order. Then recently, I started to press him to schedule articles that had been in stock for two years because they might date if not used. He published a couple, then very suddenly, he retired.

His replacement told me he was under no obligation to use them, because under their terms, the commissioning and acceptance of articles does not mean they will publish them. That felt really tough - getting photographs for some of those commissions had been a major undertaking and now they were threatening to not publish and not pay.

In total, I had 12 articles outstanding with that magazine - all commissioned by the previous editor, and many of them, written to the editor's specifications. The new editor just said, "Acceptance of articles does not guarantee publication". Two were rejected outright. The rest hang in the balance when he has time to look at them properly in the months ahead.

I'm honestly not sure if the policy has changed since his predecessor commissioned so many two years ago. It was the first I'd heard of it, but this is frustrating and it's going to be difficult to place them elsewhere as some aren't really suitable for other publications - they'll need a rewrite. It's not the first time this has happened and I'm sure it won't be the last.

One year I sold an event review to a US magazine, expecting it to be published very quickly. It was accepted, but not published. The editor said he'd let me know when it was scheduled. I didn't hear any more. When almost a year had passed, I got in touch to point out that if they didn't schedule it soon, it would be too late as the next of these annual events takes place in September! The email bounced back. He'd left and I hadn't been paid.

Trying to get hold of anyone else on the editorial team was a nightmare. But eventually I was assured they would use the piece as a preview of the event that year. It just shows how important it is to stay in touch! If I hadn't flagged the enquiry, and chased until someone came back to me, that piece would have gone unpublished and unpaid. As it turned out though, they paid very well. Do stay in touch to ensure that your work isn't forgotten!

It's a really tough environment for a freelance writer at the moment, but I'm now more choosy about who I work for and I'm starting to create new income streams. The pay cuts, I negotiate upwards as best I can. I accept the situation where I can't, and review the amount of time and effort I put into each article if they are going to pay less. If the pay is poor, I only pitch ideas that I can do reasonably quickly, without massive amounts of research and inconvenience. I also reassess who gets first refusal of the best ideas.

I refuse to work for magazines that don't treat me with respect, and I search the market to find other buyers for my work when I'm faced with non-publication of an article that was once accepted, but later unused. It's well worth being aware of alternative markets for your work in case things go wrong - as so often they do! Researching your markets and keeping up to date with what's being published is invaluable in this respect.

The constant onslaught of rejection and non-payment can be really unpleasant, especially when they've assigned you a task and you've done it in good faith. But knowing the markets thoroughly, so that you can rehome these articles helps to take the sting out of the situation and keep you smiling.

Fortunately, most editors aren't that bad. As I say, the situation has reached new levels of ridiculousness in recent years. It really is crazy, and you can either laugh about it, or you can cry. I choose to laugh, rehome articles, and work for the US magazines more and more because they're less prone to changing their minds!

Onwards and upwards. The best ways to improve your payment prospects are to:

- invoice promptly and chase regularly if they don't pay;
- try to negotiate better terms, such as payment on acceptance, if they plan to hold your article on file for a long period;
- ask them to schedule articles that have been outstanding for too long;
- and selectively work for those who treat you well.

On a more rebellious note, I have occasionally been known to withhold articles that publishers are waiting for, refusing to send them in until they've paid all their outstanding bills. That can work if you get desperate. It worked for me.

As a final measure, if they've used your work and still won't pay, there's always the small claims court. Do hang onto your commissioning emails and ensure you have the price agreed in writing, so that you know exactly what you're owed if it comes to this. Even those publications that can't commit to a firm price will be able to give you a page rate at the time of commission - a rate based on how many pages your article fills when its been set out by their designer. I looked into the small claims court once, when I was having real difficulty getting paid, and the process isn't as scary or as costly as it sounds.

Tax
What do these payment challenges mean for a writer's tax bills? Sadly, in the UK, it means you may have to pay tax on income that you haven't received yet. The situation has improved recently with a simplified cash-based option on self-assessment. However, once you're earning enough to pay more than £1000 per annum in income tax, you'll have to pay the following year's tax in advance of submitting your next return. This is when you might end up paying tax on income that you haven't received yet. It's called 'payment on account'.

There is a 10 month window between the end of the tax year on 5 April and the self assessment deadline on 31 January the following year. 'Payments on account' are due in January and July. If you're not expecting it, this comes as a nasty shock the first year when you suddenly have two payments due in January, not one.

HMRC are keen to point out that by January you should have been paid for the work you did up to 5 April in the previous year. That's wishful thinking from people who have the financial security of monthly pay cheques - but rules are rules and trying to argue with HMRC seems pretty futile to me.

However, by the time you've paid your tax in advance, you should have some of the money coming in from your articles, and with any luck, your tax will be relative to your income, so you won't be out of pocket. But just in case, a buffer is helpful. You need to keep enough in reserves to pay your tax bills when they're due or you'll end up being fined for late payment.

To be honest, it's a good idea to have reserves (or a second income) anyway, because the delays in publication and payment (not to mention those editors who change their minds) can cause havoc with your finances.

Good luck!

Chapter 23
Tips for success!

Do your research and keep pitching
Launching a career as a freelance writer isn't easy. You need to be extremely dedicated, determined, and put considerable time and effort into making your dream come true. I spent ages in newsagents, researching the markets, and pitching ideas to editors relentlessly, all day, every day. Then my first commission came in – followed by another, and another. My writing career had begun.

Maximise productivity
Pitch at least one idea every day. With a bit of luck, that should keep the work coming in. Have lots of projects on the go, so you're always productive. Stay focused on one project all morning/afternoon because multitasking can be detrimental to concentration. If you shelve a project while waiting for people to come back to you, make sure you have other projects that you can work on.

Manage deadlines
Don't leave your work outstanding until the deadline. Be disciplined and focus on getting the job done in good time. You'll get a sense of satisfaction from completing a project, and it's a good discipline to get on with your work. It also allows time for any editing and polishing that might be beneficial before the deadline. This will improve your focus and productivity. It also means that if you get an assignment with a short deadline, you're more likely to be able to fit it in.

Don't be afraid to work long hours and to work at weekends if necessary. If you really want to be a full-time freelance writer, you won't consider any deadline to be unreasonable. You'll consider it a privilege to get the work!

Manage slow periods productively
I think most writers experience slow periods. I certainly do. I make money during slow periods by pitching relentlessly, sending articles on spec to publications that usually accept my speculative work, and writing letters to magazines that pay for them. The slow period

usually ends pretty quickly when the pitching pays off and commissions start rolling in.

Even during slow periods, be disciplined. Get up early and pitch every day. Don't overlook opportunities in readers' columns, and opportunities to sell photography. Use the time to research the markets, develop your book proposals, or build your website. You can also send articles on spec to some publications. Write your blog, keep pitching, and be aware of other opportunities such as freelance websites like www.elance.com and www.thecontentcloud.net. These activities will help you make good use of slow periods.

Juggle your writing priorities

I juggle my priorities, first by deadline, and then by commitment shown by the editor. A firm commission will always take priority over something requested 'on spec', which tends to get done when I've run out of work and am tired of pitching. I don't do much 'on spec' these days because I'm usually pretty busy.

Priorities are also dictated by how easy an article is to write, how much information I'm waiting for from third parties, the availability of interviewees, and how much I value the publication itself. My favourite editors always get my best attention.

I have occasionally prioritised a non-urgent job just to get it out of the way. One of these was a speculative article for an Australian magazine who kept changing their minds about what they wanted. I was fed up with it!

Stay motivated

One of the biggest challenges to any freelance writer is discipline and motivation to get their head down and get the work done - or worse, generate the work because there isn't any!

The threat of having to get a more conventional job is my greatest motivator. I've never been cut out for a corporate office environment, yet circumstances dictated that I had to spend 20 years in those kinds of roles. Now I am highly motivated never to go back! You need to be highly motivated to succeed in this line of work.

Engage with other writers

One of my favourite parts of my first writing book is the chapter made up of contributions from other writers. It was fascinating to hear what other writers are doing in the fields of health, food and gardens. I interviewed six writers - two worked in health writing, two in food writing, and two in gardening writing. It ended up being, for me, one of the most interesting parts of the book!

I'm also fascinated by some of the successes I've seen from people in my local writers' group. It's great to engage with other writers and find out what works for them.

Have a disciplined routine

I sit down and write from 8am to 6pm every week day. I don't spend time procrastinating or worrying about writer's block. If I can't think how to get started, I just write drivel - then I return to it later to improve upon my drivel. Eventually it turns into something good. I am very disciplined. I have to be, or I'd never get anything done.

I do jot down ideas to return to later. When I'm working on a book it usually ends up as a muddle of ideas - a bit of a brain dump. It takes a lot of sorting out later! I write books in my spare time (evenings and weekends) because I don't want books to detract from my feature writing in the daytime.

Don't believe the limiting myths

People often don't take writers seriously and perpetuate limiting myths about writing as a profession. Don't let them destroy your dreams. The myth that writing is too competitive, so you might as well give up now, is no way to succeed in anything. I didn't believe it then, and I don't believe it now. The idea that you need a journalism qualification to be a journalist has also been disproven by my own experience. Essentially, believing these myths can hold you back for years. I let some of them hold me back for far too long. Don't be held back by the limiting beliefs of other people.

Engage with PR professionals

As a writer, it can be beneficial to be well connected to PR people because the news they send out provides inspiration for feature ideas. PR professionals can help you with valuable contacts too. As a published writer, you may receive invitations to press events that can lead to inspiration. That's how I got invited to Waddesdon Manor's grand Christmas opening this year. It's good to be well connected as it can lead to ideas and opportunities that can advance your writing career.

Chapter 24
Organising your workload

As your workload grows, you need to be very well organised to keep on top of your deadlines, invoicing, and to work out what's being published, where, and when. It can become quite mind boggling when you're busy and it's important to keep records for your tax return too.

I keep spreadsheets of all the writing commissions I get and record the following information in columns:

- Article title
- Commissioning publication
- Deadline
- Submission date
- Commissioning editor's name
- Email address
- Anticipated fee
- Anticipated date of publication
- Date the invoice was issued
- Date invoice was paid.

I then file all the commissioning emails in an e-folder, so that I have them to hand if I need to check anything. This helps me keep track of my work and what's outstanding in terms of my commitments, mostly editorial deadlines - and the publisher's commitments, such as scheduling and payment.

I also have a three-way check on invoices. I produce an invoice for each article once payment is due. Then when payment comes through, I file the invoice in the 'paid' folder, mark the date the money came in on the commissions spreadsheet, and add the payment to my accounts spreadsheet (which is the definitive one used when I file my tax return).

If there's a remittance advice, this goes in my expenses and receipts folder. I find this three-way check really helpful, because if I need to check what's been paid for, and when, it's all there.

Some publications don't require invoices so there's no invoice to file, but the payment still goes down in the accounts and on the commissions spreadsheet as 'invoice paid'.

If I get distracted, mid-process and fail to log something, this system is pretty foolproof. When a query comes up later, I check to see if any parts of the process were completed - if they were, it usually means the invoice was paid (I can double check the remittance folder and check my bank statements if I'm unsure), then I just need to ensure my records are aligned.

This might seem over-complicated, but it works for me. I produce about 170 feature articles in a year + 50 newspaper reports - that's just over three articles and one report every week. I need to ensure I get paid for them all, and that time-critical articles aren't missed in the publisher's schedule. Add to that, those features held back from previous years, and you can see that good organisational skills are very beneficial.

Splitting the payments between work produced in different financial years (which is necessary for filing the tax return) can become confusing if you're not well organised, but it's not complicated. Just keep impeccable records and you should be fine.

I also have a separate business bank account that helps to keep everything tidy, in anticipation that one day my accounts might be subject to an inspection by HMRC.

Keeping track of your editorial contacts and pitches

Many writers keep databases of their editorial contacts, detailing what's been pitched to whom and when. I use Excel and Word - primarily because when I started, I didn't have a database on my computer. It doesn't matter what method or software you use, but it's helpful to keep a record of your editorial contacts and what's been pitched to whom. My editorial contacts are in a spreadsheet, and my pitches are saved in Word documents, along with the date that each pitch was submitted to a publication.

It's also useful to keep a list of all your PR and interview contacts, so that you have their details to hand at the click of a mouse. I save these on a spreadsheet too.

I have Word documents, full of pitches that I've sent out over four years, along with records of who they've been sent to. These are still useful documents to refer to when I'm feeling uninspired and looking for some ideas to pitch to new publications. These documents are each labelled by topic area, which enables me to find what I need quickly.

You'll find your own way of working, but good record-keeping can make your life a lot easier. It'll mean you have the information you need to hand, when you need it. This can save you many frustrated hours of going back through emails, trying to find that little piece of information that you're sure you had six months ago, and wouldn't have deleted... you hope!

ALCS Paperwork

Once you're regularly published, you should be registering your work with the Authors Licensing and Collecting Society who pay out photocopying royalties to writers and authors twice a year on articles and books. It's remarkable how much you can earn.

One lady in our writers' group received over £2000 for a series of medical articles she had written. I received almost as much for my work in popular magazines going back three years. It's taxable income that should be declared on your tax return.

ALCS registration costs £25, but only if you earn that much, and then it's deducted from your first royalty payment, so you really can't lose.

Organisational skills are beneficial here too. You need to keep a record of all the articles you've had published in the UK, going back three years. Only UK publications with ISSN numbers are eligible and you'll need the ISSN number to register your claim. The magazine title is not sufficient. The ALCS database is outdated - many of the titles have changed and the publishers have changed. To add to the confusion, many magazines with identical names are listed - some are published overseas and not even eligible for payments. This all makes it a bit of a minefield, and that's why the ISSN is important.

The ISSN number is the one element that doesn't change. The ISSN is hidden in the bar code. Ignore the first three numbers and the last two - that gives you the ISSN number. Except for the last digit, which is sometimes different, and sometimes the same.

The ALCS website encourages you to list all your articles for a single publication in one batch, but when you have hundreds to register, it can be difficult to remember whether you have listed them all. The bulk listing method shows up as one entry, so you can't go back and check if something you think you might have forgotten is missing.

That's why I've started listing them all individually in recent years. Then I can double check what was included and what wasn't. The alternative approach is to keep a spreadsheet that records exactly what you listed, but then you might as well list them one at a time. You don't want to claim twice for a payment - that would be fraud - but you don't want to miss out on your dues either, so if you're prone to thinking you might have forgotten something, list them individually, so that you can check.

The deadline for making claims is the end of November each year. You need to double check whether the December editions (often published in November) made it into the last claim, or whether you need to add them into the next one. This is when it's really useful to have each item listed individually.

When you list an item, you will see that the publication is then greyed out. If you want to add another article, published in the same publication, just type the ISSN into the ISSN box again (or copy and paste) and this reactivates it so that you can add your next article.

www.alcs.co.uk

DACS Payback

Once you start selling photography with your work, you may also feel it's worthwhile registering for DACS Payback, which pays out royalties for photocopying artwork and photographs.

DACS Payback claims require good organisational skills too. You need to record every single photograph you have taken, that you own the copyright to, which was published in magazines going back indefinitely until the end of the previous year. In summer 2014, I claimed for my photographs when they were printed in publications up to the end of 2013. You need to be able to identify which magazines contained which photographs and provide evidence on request. Photographs obtained from other people to complement your articles are not eligible, and headshots of yourself are not eligible, even if you used your camera's timer to take the photo.

I keep a spreadsheet to show which of my photos appeared where, on what date, and I keep a record of what I have claimed. Remember to claim only for the photos published in the previous year (or earlier) and resist the urge to register your photographic work published in the current year. You can register that next year!

www.dacs.org.uk/for-artists/payback

Public Lending Rights

The Public Lending Rights Scheme pays authors for the lending of their works. If you are a commercially published author, you should register your work there too.

www.plr.uk.com

Part 3: Writing Books

This section isn't going to go into the nitty gritty of character formation or point of view - you need a specialist fiction guide for that. This part tells you what to expect in book publishing and then looks at the options for those seeking a book deal.

We'll start by looking at how to get that evasive literary agent - something you'll need if you're striving to be snapped up by a big publisher. Then we'll look at my experiences with book publishers, some options in self-publishing and a self-publishing success story that's really close to home. We'll cover writers' block, productivity, getting your brain in tip-top condition, and how to boost creativity.

You may have come across National Novel Writing Month. In this section we discuss whether it's a mug's game or a useful discipline. Then we look at marketing for your book, social media, online forums, book launches, press coverage of your book, talks and presentations, the power of the web, social media, and writing as therapy. Phew!

Then you can relax and browse the writers' resources section.

Chapter 25
Book publishing

Having a book published is the dream of many writers, but it's notoriously difficult to get a publishing deal and it's even more difficult getting good terms, unless you're rich and famous. This chapter looks at some of the options for clinching a traditional deal, as well as discussing other routes into book publishing.

Getting an agent

Having an agent dramatically increases your chances of getting a publishing deal with a big publisher. It also increases your chances of getting a decent financial offer from a publisher, so it can be worthwhile if you're serious about getting books published and making good money from them. Agents however, do come with a cost - typically between 10 and 20 percent of your book earnings.

If you send your work on spec to an agent, the acceptance rate is typically about 1 in 500. One way to, perhaps, increase the chances of your manuscript getting the attention it deserves, is to meet an agent face to face and see if they like your idea. It might also help if you hit it off with them on a personal level. Agents can be found at publishing shows like the London Book Fair.

The Writers' and Artists' Yearbook, The Australian Writers' Marketplace, or The Writers' Market in the USA, has a list of agents and their specialties. In some cases, they provide details of the authors on their books, and their fees.

Check out agents who deal with the subject you're writing about, and look at their website for submission guidelines. Targeting agents who deal in your genre is a vast improvement upon randomly contacting agents, many of whom may never deal in the topics covered by your book!

It can also be worthwhile looking at new titles in the book shops and when you see something similar to your own, see if you can find out which agent the publisher uses. They may be in the market for similar material.

Getting an agent isn't easy, but if you get one that's well connected and believes in your work, they can be worth their weight in gold!

The direct approach

If you do decide to approach a publisher directly, then the usual rule of thumb is to provide a synopsis of your proposed book, including a chapter breakdown, and the first few chapters as a taster of what is to come. Those publishers who do deal directly with authors will usually provide details of their exact requirements, either online, or on request.

It can take months for publishers to respond to proposals, so you need to be patient, but don't be put off if one publisher turns you down. It often takes multiple attempts to get an idea accepted. Most best selling authors have suffered rejection, but they are famous now because they didn't give up, and eventually they got the break they needed.

There are a few publishers who have schemes specifically for new writers. One such publisher is Jonathan Cape, part of Random House Publishing, who during 'Cape Open Submissions' every June (at the time of writing), accept online submissions of manuscripts for consideration by their publishing team. They require the first 50 pages of your manuscript, and say, "These can be part of a novel or novella, or short stories. The pages can be finished work or a work in progress." It doesn't matter what font type, size, or spacing you use in your 50 page manuscript - the submission is just to give them a feel for your work. If they're interested in seeing more, they'll get in touch. www.vintage-books.co.uk/capesubmissions

Harper Collins' website for new authors, www.authonomy.com, enables writers to upload their manuscripts for review. Visitors to the website comment on the works and rank each contribution, and if your book gets good feedback, then Harper Collins will look at it with a view to possibly offering you a book deal.

Pan MacMillan has a 'MacMillan New Writing Scheme', but at the time of writing it is closed to new submissions. One to watch perhaps? www.panmacmillan.com/Imprints

Tinder Open Submissions accepts fiction manuscripts from writers who have never had a novel published. Tinder Press is a division of Headline Publishing. www.tinderpress.co.uk

Magic Oxygen Books is a small publisher who is willing to talk directly to new authors and will consider manuscripts written by people who don't have an agent. www.magicoxygen.co.uk

My experiences with a small publisher

John Hunt Publishing has an unusual approach to publishing, which has attracted much controversy and criticism over the years. They started in 2001 with one imprint, O Books, and expanded to include new imprints covering spiritual and religious titles, freelance writing, fiction, history, the paranormal, and self-help topics.

Despite reading some unflattering reviews about the publisher, I gave them the benefit of the doubt a few years ago and accepted a 'level 2' contract to write a new title, 'Freelance Writing on Health, Food and Gardens' for their writing imprint, Compass Books.

Unlike most traditional publishers, John Hunt Publishing will consider titles that may not have mass market appeal and may sell in relatively small numbers compared to larger publishers. This is a bonus for new writers who are looking for a way into publishing, but have little in the way of a public profile or a committed following. It may also be suitable for those who want to write about a niche subject that has limited appeal.

The model works well for aspiring authors who want to go the traditional publishing route, but have been unable to get a conventional book deal because they're deemed too high-risk or not commercial enough for a traditional publisher.

John Hunt Publishing look at the first chapter of your proposed book and the chapter breakdown. They will make a decision on those works alone. Three of their experts give a view on your proposal and offer their comments. These are fed back through the online database that they use to communicate with applicants and authors.

John Hunt Publishing have many different levels of contract, and if you are offered one of the first two levels, they publish the book and pay you royalties at 10 to 25 percent of net receipts on paperbacks. There is no advance paid, but royalties are paid out at six monthly intervals.

If you're offered a contract at level three or lower, there is an author contribution to be paid, should you decide to accept it. This is quite unusual, except among the vanity press, but John Hunt Publishing, insist that they are not a vanity publisher.

John Hunt Publishing use a central database for communicating with their authors and if you have a query, you have to raise it in the online forum, rather than with the staff directly. This helps to channel queries to the correct person, and keeps costs down. From the author's perspective, it is a mixed experience. The answers provided in the forum are sometimes unsatisfactory. Sometimes you don't get an answer at all! If you're a bit of a rebel, you can usually get hold of someone by email, but they'd rather you didn't!

One of the unexpected 'delights' of being an author with this publisher, is their propensity to do 99p promotions, whether you like it or not. At 99p, your ebook royalties - 50% of net receipts - sink to almost nothing. I'm not sure how this discounting practice benefits either the author or the publisher, but my guess is, they hope people will buy more Compass Books on similar topics at full price because they liked the 99p one so much!

The publishing experience has been a mix of good and bad. They have recently changed the terms so that ebook conversion costs are taken out of author royalties. This raised a few eyebrows in the early days.

If, as a writer, you want to be published in the traditional sense with the support of a publisher, with all the usual services: a proof reader/editor, graphic designer, basic PR services, and a low-level support network, then John Hunt Publishing presents a real option. If you want to make serious money, or are sensitive to, or insulted by, very low/zero royalties for months at a time, then there are probably better options to consider like traditional publishers, Kindle Direct Publishing or Amazon's CreateSpace!

The power of KDP

If traditional publishing doesn't appeal because of the difficulty getting a book deal (or the challenges of dealing with smaller publishers), why not consider self-publishing on Kindle Direct Publishing? The advantages of this approach are that it costs nothing and puts you completely in control. The disadvantages are that it's a flooded market and it's only accessible to those people with ereaders, tablets, or the desire to read books sat at a computer. However, it's also a growing market as more and more people buy reading devices and embrace the publishing revolution.

Having read reports saying that most self-published ebooks sell less than 100 copies (many less than 10!) I was sceptical about the whole thing, so I was blown away when I heard that one of our

Writers' Group members, Dave Sivers, has enjoyed five figure sales on his latest crime novels through Kindle Direct Publishing. Dave's work is always impeccable and his success with KDP made me think again. The sales are comparable to an advance from a traditional publishing house!

At the time of writing, his two 'Archer and Baines' crime novels, *The Scars Beneath the Soul* and *Dead in Deep Water*, have between them, amassed sales well into five figures and are still showing strongly in the Kindle 'Serial Killers' top 20 bestsellers chart.

His winning formula seems to consist of great writing, excellent reviews, a strong social media presence with lots of followers, and a regular readers' newsletter. His sales really exploded after he worked on improving his Twitter following, and he says, "I wish I'd done that before I published my first book!"

I asked Dave for additional insight as to how he'd achieved those remarkable sales figures, and he explained that the sales of both titles escalated when he released his second novel in the 'Archer and Baines' series, 'Dead in Deep Water'.

"I had bookmarks printed in advance and thrust them into the hands of anyone foolish enough to ask me if/what I write," he said, "which may have translated into a few purchases. And, needless to say, I've been pinching myself and sharing each new high with my long-suffering Twitter and Facebook chums, who have not only put up with it, but been incredibly supportive and pleased for me, sharing my news and helping to spread the word. I'm pretty sure that had an effect, despite reading some blog posts asserting that engaging with social media doesn't sell books.

"However, I'm sure, in many cases, that people who enjoyed the first title in the series, 'The Scars Beneath the Soul', were coming back for more. That doesn't explain everything, because, for every two copies of 'Dead in Deep Water' sold, another copy of Scars found its way onto someone's Kindle. So apparently a lot of people were finding their way to Archer and Baines through Book 2 and buying Book 1 as well; and there are plenty more out there who bought Book 1 but haven't yet found their way to Book 2.

"Perhaps the most interesting fact then, is the way ALL my titles have had such an upturn in fortunes. It does seem a fair bet that a number of readers have discovered me through the latest book and sought out more of my work.

"Of course, that increases the pressure, just a little bit, to get the next thing out there. I'm now locking myself in my garret and working in earnest on Archer and Baines Book 3, which I'm excited about already. Because, once I fall through what Stephen King calls that hole in the page and into the story, stuff like sales figures and chart rankings are forgotten."

Dave's top tips for KDP success

- Your number one objective when starting out is to build a readership and engage with them.
- A strong online presence will not guarantee success, but not having one will almost certainly guarantee failure.
- It's never too soon to start building your online presence. Don't wait until the book is already on sale. Use your online networks to create anticipation for your baby.
- Do have an online launch party. See how other people do it, rather than throwing something together. You won't have any clearing up to do either.
- A good price offer for the first book in a series is more likely to encourage readers to take a punt on a new writer. If they like book 1, they may pay a little more for book 2. But remember how price-conscious ebook readers can be.
- The big advantage you have over commercially published authors is control. Never, never, relinquish that control by, for example, making promises to readers about a publication date before the book is good to go.
- There is no need to spend a fortune on elements of the production process you can manage 'in house', using either your own skills or those of trusted friends. Be 100% honest and realistic about how good those skills really are. Your published package needs to be as good as it can possibly be.
- Amazon tells you who else your readers are reading. If you hook up with those authors and their readers on social media, those readers might check you out and like the look of your book too.
- Constantly plugging your book in social media is not engaging with people. It is spamming them.

- Have a marketing strategy. Whatever you do, growing a readership and a reputation takes time. Be ambitious, but realistic, about your goals.
- Celebrate successes - a book launch, a good review, a little milestone in sales.
- Most of the above probably applies to all but the top commercially published authors too.

Find out more about Kindle Direct Publishing here: https://kdp.amazon.com

Create Space

Amazon CreateSpace is another option for those looking to publish traditional, paperback books. The books are printed on demand, sold on Amazon online, and royalties are paid to the author for each sale. The only outlay to the author is the cost of a physical proof of the book to be posted from the USA.

You can, of course, choose the sale price and list it as an ebook too. You are completely in control of the process, which is a very nice position to be in if you're comfortable with doing all the donkey work.

The downside is that there is no professional cover designer (although Amazon's online tools will give you a helping hand), no marketing support, no proof reading/editing, and none of the other services that you get with a traditional publisher. It's quite a lot of work to self publish to a professional level, and it requires exceptional attention to detail.

Find out more about CreateSpace here: www.createspace.com

Smashwords

If you want to publish your ebook across all e-publishing platforms, including Kobo and Nook, take a look at www.smashwords.com. This website provides a one stop shop for uploading your work onto all the main publishers' ebook sites. This means that readers with any e-reading device can download your work.

Smashwords is not as straight forward as KDP and there's an instruction manual on formatting that's over 100 pages long!

However, it's not as overwhelming as it may first appear and the main rule on formatting for Smashwords is to keep it simple.

While opinions vary on the value of making your work available across different platforms, I'd suggest it's worth doing, unless you want to make your work exclusive to the Kindle Select programme. If you commit to KDP exclusivity through Kindle Select, you get 70% royalties on all geographical markets where your work is sold at $2.99 or above, and you also get royalties on borrows. But you don't know what benefits you might be missing on other platforms.

Most authors seem to think it's worth being cross-platform for a while, although many report very low sales on platforms other than Kindle. However some do well from being available across different platforms, so experiences vary enormously, which is why it's usually worth trying.

Chapter 26
Writers' block and productivity

Do you frequently suffer from writer's block? If you want to be more productive, you need to overcome that. Don't stop writing just because you hit a sticky patch. Write badly. Write rubbish. Jot down ideas. You can always improve upon your work later. Bad writing is much easier to improve upon than a blank page.

If you're having difficulty with one project, switch to writing something different, and then return to the challenging bit later. Professional writers can't afford to have writers' block. They have to press on, past the total lack of inspiration and get something down on the page, even if it's not very good.

If your story has hit a patch that is so sticky, you just can't move it forward, perhaps your story has taken a wrong turn and you need to go back to the plotting stage. Work with other writers and sort out your plot before you proceed any further. But don't stop writing. Write articles, do some blogging, pitch for new commissions, or work on your photography. Keep writing - or creating in another way - and stay productive.

Eat well and be inspired
Another thing to consider - something that you probably won't find in any other writers' book - is the power of good food on the mind. The brain needs to be well nourished to function properly. Most people are deficient in essential nutrients like omega 3. This stifles creativity and may increase your propensity to writers' block.

Omega 3 oils are beneficial oils that reduce cholesterol and clean up the arteries. They are considered to be very good for the brain and can help you concentrate. Omega 3 oils are also essential for your emotional wellbeing. They reduce your risk of depression and may enhance the creative process.

A study by French researchers Manzoni and Laye, showed that long term deficiency of omega 3 in the diet may cause mood disorders such as depression and harm your synaptic function. This could make you slow and unresponsive. Not good when you have editorial deadlines coming up. A tuna sandwich can provide omega 3 oils and other foods rich in omega 3 are walnuts, flaxseed, soy beans, and oily fish.

Brightly coloured fruits and vegetables are good for the mind too. They contain a wide range of antioxidant compounds which promote clean arteries, improve blood flow to the brain, and support concentration, creativity and decision making. Blueberries, strawberries, raspberries, oranges, broccoli, butternut squash and tomatoes, are examples of foods that are loaded with antioxidants. They're much better to nibble at your desk than chocolate!

The beneficial effects of antioxidants on the brain were demonstrated in a study where participants who consumed a cup of blueberries every day for two weeks, performed better in mental tests than the control group. The blueberries increased the number of brain cells in the hippocampus which is responsible for memory and spatial navigation.

Other nutrients that improve the flow of blood/oxygen to the brain and aid clear thinking, are potassium and folic acid. Potassium-rich foods include bananas, jacket potatoes, leafy green vegetables, sunflower seeds, and citrus fruits.

Folic acid is a great brain food, widespread in whole foods, particularly in green leafy vegetables, carrots, avocados, melons, apricots, and pumpkins, as well as beans and whole grains. The Baltimore Longitudinal Study of Aging, the longest running study of aging in the USA, found that folic acid has beneficial effects on the brain which reduce the risk of Alzheimer's disease.

If you want to power-up your brain, reach for natural whole foods. A variety of natural produce in your diet will provide you with a wide range of nutrients that support your mind. Vitamins, minerals, essential oils, antioxidants and amino acids (the building blocks of protein), all play a role in brain function and support concentration and creativity. So if you're in need of a pick-me-up in the middle of your writing day, a fish oil capsule or a punnet of strawberries might be more beneficial than a chocolate bar! You could, of course, try both!

Go for a walk!

A study published in 2014 by Stanford University showed that individuals' creative output increased after walking, whether that was walking indoors on a treadmill, or strolling in the great outdoors. Getting outdoors without exercising did not show the same benefits. Exercise was key to getting the blood pumping and the mind working optimally.

Furthermore, the researchers said that walking twice may be even more beneficial to the creative process, so if after one walk you're still struggling with your writing project, perhaps another stroll will help!

Chapter 27
National Novel Writing Month

Last year I picked up and dusted off an old ring binder containing the first half of a handwritten novel that I'd produced 20 years ago. I read it, and felt parts of it had potential, so after considerable work in getting the good bits typed up, I began a major undertaking in reworking an old idea into a modern storyline. The basic concept is good and the foundations of the story are laid, which I find quite helpful. Some of the characters are reasonably well created in my head, and I've also firmed up the plot so that the whole thing is more true to life and has a clear ending. The project ran out of steam 20 years ago and had no ending!

Now fiction is not my strongest suit, so I'm taking my time on this project - and of course, the paying work always comes first, which means it spends a lot of time on the back burner, but every November, I commit to getting on with my novel for National Novel Writing Month. This ensures the project moves forward every year... even if just a little bit.

National Novel Writing Month comes round every November and the idea is to write the first 50,000 words of your novel over the course of the month. Like me, you can work on whatever you like really, but it's an opportune time to commit to a writing project that you would otherwise, keep putting off.

Those 50,000 word novels produced every November are drafts - probably bad drafts for the most part, but it's an event bringing together almost 300,000 novelists each year, working on their own projects in sync, with a sense of community. And in that sense alone, it's motivational, and it gives you a limited time to block out all distractions and just get on with it.

Now some people dislike National Novel Writing Month, saying it's an excuse for people to write shoddy novels in a rush and self publish at the end of the month, giving self publishing a bad name. While I guess there's an element of that, for me it's something quite different.

I'll admit that when I first heard of National Novel Writing Month, I thought it sounded like a stupid idea. I mean, why wait for

November? And why try to do it in a month? You can do a better job, probably, by taking your time, and writing it carefully.

However, I've since decided that perhaps National Novel Writing Month could be a useful event after all. When I first took part, I'd been intending to tackle this half-cut unfinished novel for the past year. It had potential but was badly in need of a rewrite. On 2 November I decided to begin that rewrite. National Novel Writing Month gave me a kick up the butt to get on with it.

So to those people who say National Novel Writing Month is all about rushing to complete a shoddy piece of work. Here's my answer...

For me, it's not about rushing. I need to *prioritise* this book or it will never be written. I have a day job writing magazine articles that take priority. They continue to take priority in November, but setting myself a target to do as much as I can on evenings and weekends, gives me an incentive to prioritise it during my leisure time (which otherwise tends to get swallowed up with paying work too). That's why I joined the novelists on National Novel Writing Month. Frankly, it's also nice to have a sense of community egging you on!

That month of intense commitment moved the project onto the next stage. I now have a decent draft. By the end of National Novel Writing Month my novel was in a better place than it was at the start. I reached 38,000 words not 50,000, but I was pleased with the result, and my dedication to the project continued into December and January until I had a decent first draft of the whole manuscript. That was refreshing progress.

What did I learn?

I learnt that I should've planned better first. It was quite hard-going in places trying to keep the daily word-count up. I was still working out mini plots and doing research to establish what is, and what isn't, realistic. My whole plot almost fell apart when I discovered that clinical trials can take ten years to complete. Ten years! That messed up my whole plot entirely! Then my husband pointed out that they manage to bring out new flu vaccines very quickly, so I figure there's some flexibility around that figure.

However the aim of National Novel Writing Month, to complete 50,000 words, does assume that you've already done your research and you're not too far off working out your plot. So perhaps my lack of preparation was my downfall.

What else did I learn? Stop editing perhaps? Editing while I wrote probably didn't help either. If you decide to edit, then you probably won't reach the target. I realised this early on but decided to edit anyway. I figured that if the earlier plots weren't right, then continuing on a theme that was wrong, was just going to end up with a rubbish manuscript. I'm keen to get it right, rather than just do it fast, so I took time out for a little editing too.

For more about National Novel Writing Month visit www.nanowrimo.org

Chapter 28
Marketing, social media and online forums

Marketing is important for all authors. It's the lucky, the few, and the famous who get big marketing budgets from their publishers. The rest of us have to muck in and spread the word! So get to it!

A Book Launch
If your book is a novel or a non-fiction title with wide appeal, a launch event at your local bookshop or library might be a worthwhile activity. You can invite friends, relatives, press, dignitaries, and anyone on your mailing list who might be interested.

Jane Wenham-Jones, in her book, *Wannabe a Writer We've Heard Of?* admits that launch parties don't sell many books, but she adds that they can be a good promotional tool if you take a radical approach! The key, apparently, is to have a memorable theme that will raise a few eyebrows...

"If you've written that book about lap dancers and have a few of them strutting their stuff throughout the evening, I can guarantee you a few column inches," she says, in her own unique style! Jane also suggests that your press launch should include: wine, nibbles, a celebrity guest if possible, "or anyone remotely famous". Then you socialise, do a short speech and conclude with book signing and more socialising until home time.

Media coverage
Getting coverage of your book in relevant media is definitely worth some effort. I write for the popular writing magazines in the UK and take the opportunity to plug my books at the end of my articles, alongside the author biography.

If you have a traditional publisher, then they'll probably do a lot of the publicity for you, but if you're self publishing, you can perhaps get coverage by engaging with reviewers personally. Follow some book reviewers on social media, take an interest in what they do, and at an opportune time, mention your book, and see if they have the time, interest and inclination to review it for you!

If you don't have a publisher taking care of press releases, you might want to send your own press release to relevant magazines, with the offer of a review copy if they'd like to cover it in their publication. Your back cover copy should be compelling enough to make them want to read on, so you shouldn't need to add a lot, except perhaps what makes it current, exciting, and a 'must have' for their readers.

If, like me, you write for magazines, there might be opportunities to promote your book at the conclusion of your article - especially if your book is related to the topic covered in the article. I recently wrote an article for Writing Magazine about making money in writing and promoted one of my books as part of the feature. It was great to receive a call from a lady who had ordered the book on the basis of that article. I also received a tweet from someone who said the article was really inspiring.

Look out for free literary magazines that are looking for content too. I promote my first book regularly in Compass Books' free magazine, 'Writers' Wheel', which is usually open to receive submissions from their own authors. I also write blogs that help to promote my books, while giving the reader some useful tips to help them move forward in their writing career.

Talks and presentations

Literary festivals and writers' groups are always looking for speakers to talk about books and the writing process. You might also find opportunities to do book signings at local events where crowds of people will be present. These can work well if your book has wide appeal.

If you're not used to public speaking, it can be a good idea to start small while you practise to increase your confidence. You might like to consider joining a speakers' society or toastmaster's club, which will help to develop your skills as a proficient public speaker.

Speaking for the first time, even to a modest group, can be daunting. When I delivered a talk to my local writers' group, I was completely chilled about the whole experience until about two hours before I was due to speak, at which point, I suddenly got nervous, sweaty, and my mind went blank! Fortunately, I'd made extensive notes to jog my memory in anticipation of that happening!

At the event, I covered my work history in marketing before leaping into the crazy, but rewarding, world of freelance writing. I showed the audience the first article I'd had published in The Lady, 19 years earlier, and the nutrition articles that I'd written for free to help develop a small portfolio. This helped to launch my freelance writing career in 2011.

Then I showed them my magazine articles and explained the inspiration behind some of the ideas. This helped because I could focus on the magazines and the work, rather than on my speaking proficiency! People seemed interested and asked about it, which helped the flow and helped me to relax into the process.

Feeling a little more comfortable, I outlined my daily writing discipline and routine, and explained how my husband supports me as a proof-reader, photographer, chauffeur, and second memory! I told them about the days when I sat in the garden with a huge pile of magazines, making notes on what I could potentially write that would be suitable for each publication. I'd spent hours generating ideas for features and then pitching A-Z through the Writers and Artists Yearbook. I hung around magazine stands a lot in those days. I pitched to niche titles and I thought very widely about opportunities.

Then I explained how to write a winning pitch – the hook, expertise, photos, why you're the right person to write the piece, and examples of your work and your clients. I even talked about marketing yourself as a writer by demonstrating your experience, making sure you have a good web presence, social media and blogs to promote your work.

I talked about how I found inspiration in unusual places, and shared lots of the articles I'd written in the first few years - covering local topics, interviewing local people, and studying the markets for inspiration. Turning rejections into sales and avoiding legal issues seemed to go down well with some discussion around libel, copyright, and avoiding controversy.

Getting paid was perhaps one of the more lively discussions. We often work well ahead of publication, and have to wait until after publication to see the money come in. I explained how I'd overcome non-payers by holding back the next article until they'd paid for the last four, or simply harassing them into submission. Then to conclude, I talked about photography, speculative submissions, and writing for pleasure.

The talk was essentially an outline of my book, 'Freelance Writing on Health, Food and Gardens'. I sold three copies - not quite as many as I'd hoped, but you can't win them all. I've been advised that the next time I do a talk, I should charge!

Take part in a blog hop!

In 2014 I was invited to participate in a 'blog hop', entitled 'My Writing Process'. These blog hops were all over Twitter at the time. They're designed to generate interest in the work of authors and raise their profiles. I had to respond to a series of questions about my work in progress, genre, inspiration and writing discipline. It might not send your sales spiralling, but every little helps! You can see mine at: www.susiekearley.blogspot.co.uk/2014/03/blog-hop-my-writing-process.html

The power of the web

The growth of the Internet is changing the face of publishing and challenging those who work within the industry to adapt and keep up with the speed of new technology. It's a mixed blessing for publishers, who are seeing competition escalate, the readerships of traditional print publishing decline, and they're facing totally new challenges in the dynamic and ever-changing, digital publishing world. Availability of free news over the Internet is a real threat to traditional print publishing, but on the upside, the internet has opened up lucrative opportunities in e-publishing, and for people like you and me, it has slashed the time and cost of pitching ideas to publications, which is amazing news. I really hated having to print off query letters and spend all my money on stamps when I first started testing the freelance market back in the 1990s!

The Internet has opened up quick and easy access to research opportunities, and made accessing new markets for your work easier than ever before. It has also created the opportunity to showcase your work online, build a reputation online, and to self-publish at virtually no expense.

A website is something that all ambitious writers should use to demonstrate their expertise. It may even help you to clinch that evasive publishing deal. I received a book deal purely on the basis of my website content. It was designed to show editors that I'm a widely-published writer, on a diverse range of topics and specialist areas - but I never expected to get a book deal from it.

The publisher could see that I had expertise writing about health, food and gardens, because at that time, I had hundreds of articles on those topics available for download from my website.

The website still serves as a good shop window. There are many free website building tools online, so it you're reasonably proficient on a computer, you can build your own website, as they're pretty intuitive. Here are some of the templated DIY sites that don't cost anything for a basic website: www.wix.com, www.weebly.com, www.yola.com, www.moonfruit.com, www.uk.webs.com, and www.sites.google.com.

Author interviews

My publisher's PR team arranged an author interview with Women on Writing, to sit alongside a book review. I've also taken part in interviews on writers' blogs, speaking to Elaine Spires, Jennifer Bohnet, and Hywela Lyn Evans about everything from my favourite holidays to my writing inspirations! I came runner-up in a 'writer of the year' competition and took part in an author interview for that too. Interviews are a good way to engage with other writers and build contacts, while giving your book a plug and raising your profile.

Build a social media profile

The explosion of social media use on smart phones, combined with its widening appeal across all age groups, presents an unprecedented opportunity to engage with your audience. For some, social media is no longer a nice-to-have part of their promotional mix: many publishers consider it essential.

The direct and interactive nature of social media makes it both cost-effective and powerful, providing the opportunity to engage with readers, editors, and the wider publishing community, sharing your successes and showcasing your work.

The greatest strength of social media is also its greatest challenge – the open interaction and the potential for negativity. Experts say this shouldn't put you off because it benefits you to know what people are saying - both the good and the bad, so that you can take the feedback into account for future projects! You can't please everyone and you may need to block persistent pests, but fortunately for writers, the vast majority of feedback you receive is likely to be positive... unless you're deliberately controversial and then anything could happen!

One thing that works well on social media, is humour. If your posts make people smile, they often share them, and your posts can go viral very quickly. This is particularly so of video clips, but viral marketing is not limited to humour – anything that has widespread appeal and followers want to share with their friends has the potential to go viral. This is an extremely good way to reach a large audience quickly, and you'll often gain more followers as a direct result of a successful viral marketing campaign.

Social media is an extension of your publisher's PR team. By checking your account daily and posting valuable content, you will enhance your profile and generate lasting fans that benefit your reputation and hopefully build your profile and your book sales. Don't be afraid to try something different if your current approach is not having the desired effect.

Good practice tips:
- Help people find your social media sites by putting links on your website, on the foot of emails, and on other communications.
- Take time to nurture relationships, provide content that your audiences value and don't overtly market yourself or your books. A gentle approach is more effective.
- You can use your followers as a focus group to provide feedback on ideas.
- People like to share laughter and anguish. Give them laughter and try to keep anguish to a minimum by being supportive and encouraging.
- Post often and enjoy it, but don't spend so long on social media that it cuts into your writing time.

The most popular social media platforms

Twitter: There are mixed of views on whether you should follow everyone back on Twitter and build a following of thousands that way, or whether it's better to follow and engage with a handful of quality contacts. I prefer the latter approach, but I know authors who swear that following back in huge numbers (and following others in the hope that they follow you) has helped to raise their profile, and crucially, to sell their books.

Facebook: Facebook makes it increasingly difficult for followers to see the posts on author pages. Typically, a post onto an author page will only reach about 10% of the people following your page. For this reason, authors are increasingly abandoning author fan pages, in favour of collecting 'friends' on their private accounts instead. To be honest, if you want to keep your private account private - for interactions with people you actually know - managing an author page on Facebook may not be the best use of your time. Facebook is driven by advertising revenues, and they want you to advertise. If you don't spend money, your page gets very little exposure.

YouTube: Making a video to create interest in your book can be beneficial. Any method of engaging with readers in new and innovative ways online can help to generate interest in your work.

Other social media that are fast gaining popularity include GooglePlus, StumbleUpon, Tumblr, and Goodreads. I've seen someone get bullied on Goodreads and heard that it's a bit of a problem, so treat with caution, although I've also heard that the groups on Goodreads are excellent for engaging with readers in a way that promotes your books.

This brings me nicely onto the next topic: feedback. When you start to engage with other writers, you may be drawn into giving and receiving feedback on each other's work or ideas. This can go badly wrong, but equally it can provide inspiration for articles. The next chapter is a reprint of an article inspired by a cyber-bullying attack that I witnessed on Facebook. It provided inspiration for a piece that was published in Writers' Forum magazine in 2013.

Chapter 29
How to give constructive feedback

I was astonished. Why would anyone be so nasty to a complete stranger? This online discussion had gone way too far!

It was a web-based forum designed to support writers, but my jaw dropped as one poor contributor was accused of being 'over-sensitive', getting an 'attack of the vapours', and told there would be negative reviews - all under the guise of constructive feedback!

This bitter exchange ended sharply when the moderator threatened to ban both parties from the group.

While personal attacks are clearly not constructive, the discussion made me think about the best approaches to giving and receiving constructive feedback in a variety of situations. I spoke to other writers and writing tutors to gauge their opinions, both on giving feedback, and on how to handle a disappointing critique. Their thoughts on this controversial topic were fascinating.

But let's begin with my own personal experience. As a young aspiring author over 20 years ago, I enrolled on a writing correspondence course where the assignments were delivered by post. I had a tutor called Stephen, whose feedback was simply dreadful. I still have the assignments and looking back at them, I'm not surprised I gave up!

Stephen's feedback on one assignment read, "This just isn't how it's done." That was it. He didn't offer any advice on how my work might be improved. He didn't bother to tell me what was wrong with it. And because all assignments were submitted by post, with no system in place to respond to feedback, there was little opportunity for further discussion.

I gave up, but the course came with a lifetime guarantee. So I resumed the course 20 years later in 2011, and was assigned a new tutor. When I submitted my first assignment, I received 30 pages of detailed feedback - all of which was helpful, positive, and valuable going forward. What a transformation! I also queried a couple of things he said by email and we ended up having a discussion about the omniscient perspective in my fiction.

This is the most stark example I've experienced to date, of how positive, helpful feedback can move a project forward, while unhelpful feedback can be devastating and literally stop a writer in their tracks!

Other writers gave me their thoughts and experiences...

Sandra Smith, Writing Tutor

Freelance writer and writing tutor, Sandra Smith, had a similar experience. She said, "On the first writing course I attended my tutor was scathing about a short story I'd written. At the end of the weekend, several groups amalgamated and I was the only person not invited to read aloud pieces they had worked on, even though the tutor had praised one of my poems (which went on to be published). Looking back, my storyline was weak but it took me a long time to overcome such humiliation. There's no way I'd inflict that on anyone else!"

Today, Sandra uses a much more constructive approach with her own students, "As a creative writing tutor, constructive feedback is a crucial element of all my teaching. Writers come to me because they want to learn and improve. So I see my role as twofold: to praise and develop those areas where the writer shows natural skill (this might be realistic dialogue or compelling characters); and nurture the weaker areas. The latter is perhaps where too many are tempted to criticise, but how does criticism help the writer? If they have settled for an ending that is predictable, then show examples of how a last-minute twist could surprise the reader - or brainstorm ideas and cultivate their imagination so they are persuaded to think beyond the obvious."

Read more about Sandra's work on her website: www.TheCurrentMrsSmith.co.uk

Nancy O'Neill, author

I spoke to Nancy O'Neill, author of Guess What Books for children, and she said, "When you're giving feedback on someone's work, sometimes just the choice of words makes a difference. For example, if you want to suggest the author develop their characters more, instead of saying "the characters lack substance or interest," you could say, "what if you..." or "it might help to..." Just the words, "what if" and "might" can make feedback sting a little less, especially for new writers. Also, instead of criticism, you've now given them a new idea which hopefully they'll be more likely to consider. I work with authors in developing their writing skills. Helping them to improve their story is a delicate balance."

See Nancy's books on: www.guesswhatbooks.com

Simon Whaley, author and writing tutor

Simon Whaley is a freelance writer, blogger, and author of 15 books including The Positively Productive Writer. He is also a course tutor with The Writers Bureau.

Simon says: "When giving constructive feedback the word 'because' becomes important. For example: that opening paragraph doesn't work because... (or that opening paragraph works brilliantly because...). If I say to a student that their opening paragraph doesn't work, and I leave it at that, I've given them no advice on how to improve it. But if I say their opening paragraph doesn't work because it doesn't explain to the reader what their article is about, then they have something to build on. Constructive feedback points a writer in the right direction, towards the solution.

"However, constructive feedback isn't just about pointing out the weaknesses. I believe a tutor should point out strengths too, explaining why something works well. I try to ensure that for every comment I make explaining why something doesn't work in their writing, I always include one that shows where they're doing something right. That way, I hope I offer encouragement to a student, as well as guidance on how they can improve their work. By telling someone how to improve their piece of work, you're also giving them the encouragement that it can be improved."

On the topic of receiving feedback

Simon says, "When it comes to reading through a critique of your work, read it once then put it aside. Sometimes you may not like what you read, but the initial anger can cloud rational thought. Leave it a couple of days and then reread it. You are likely to be more receptive to any suggestions the critique offers.

"If you are receiving a critique in a face-to-face group environment, such as at a writers' group, write down people's comments. That does two things: it records the advice being offered, so that you can reflect upon it later, and it also occupies you! If you don't write it down, you are more likely to answer your critics, increasing the risk of the critiquing session becoming a confrontation. When you begin answering your critics with phrases like, "No, what I meant there was ..." you're demonstrating that your writing hasn't conveyed the message you wanted it to, so you're trying to explain it now. A writer should remember that they may not always be there, beside their reader, to explain what they really meant. Concentrating on writing down feedback forces you to listen to what is being said.

"If there's anything you don't understand, always ask for clarification and an example. Not only does this ensure that you understand the point they're making, but it also makes the feedback more constructive. Constructive feedback should motivate a writer to improve their work."

Read more about Simon's work on his website: www.simonwhaley.co.uk

So now you're interested in online forums?
The internet is abundant with vibrant communities where writers gather to discuss ideas, comment on best practice, get views on personal challenges, and gauge the opinions of other writers on their work. These forums can be extremely valuable, providing access to a like-minded community, each sharing ideas and inspiration.

For the most-part, writers are supportive of one another's work, providing helpful feedback and good ideas. Members often share poems, competitions, blogs, book extracts, and discuss challenges.

If you're interested in joining an online discussion forum, there are many to choose from on Facebook, LinkedIn, or Google Plus. One of my favourite sites is Twitter, where writers connect with other writers, sharing blogs, ideas and making friends along the way. There are also dedicated sites for writers, and some of these are listed below.

www.writerscafe.org
www.writers-online.co.uk
www.scribophile.com
www.greatwriting.co.uk
www.writers-network.com
www.youngwritersonline.net

Just remember that if you find yourself in receipt of personal attacks online, ignore them and discuss your writing in a different forum instead, where the feedback is more constructive. Responding to personal attacks can be a downhill journey.

Unhelpful feedback:
- That's rubbish!
- That's a stupid idea.
- It's boring.
- I don't like it.
- You obviously don't understand.
- That's just not how it's done.

Constructive feedback:
- Explain how a scene might be portrayed more effectively.
- Offer ideas that might improve the piece of work.
- Explain why you think a piece of writing is not working, and offer suggestions for improvement (This isn't working for me, because… but it could be improved by…).

Chapter 30
Writing as therapy

This book is about writing as a profession, but there are people who manage to combine therapeutic writing with good earnings. Just look at the explosion of gut-wrenching memoirs that have hit the bookshelves in recent years.

Many people have been drawn to the writing craft through feelings of being different or rejected, and because they want to be able to express themselves freely and without criticism. They learn to craft their feelings onto paper and sometimes this approach not only tells a great story, but it can be psychologically healing, and even quite profound. It's a way of analyzing everything that's happened to you, and understanding how it's shaped the person you've become. It can also help other people who are struggling with similar issues in their lives.

Writing is often adopted as a therapeutic tool by people who are prone to depression because it allows them to express themselves in a non-threatening way. They don't get judged and they don't have to share their thoughts if they don't want to. A number of the writers on Twitter are very open about their depression. Some harness their feelings to write powerful literature, full of raw emotion and hard truths. Some of this work is very good. It comes straight from the heart and it challenges the status quo in our society, which frankly, sometimes needs to be challenged.

There is a lot of research showing that writing can be therapeutic and beneficial to people suffering from trauma. It can even be beneficial to those suffering from everyday stress, to help them work through their day-to-day challenges.

Therapeutic writing offers a way of getting your emotions out into the open, providing a release mechanism for suppressed feelings, which may have been bottled up for years. It may help reveal solutions to problems, or identify new ways of coping with difficult feelings.

Even the editing process is said to be therapeutic, because you can hone and perfect the words until you're completely comfortable with the message portrayed. That's something you can't do in talk therapy when you might express something badly and later wish you'd expressed it differently... or perhaps not said it at all.

Honing your writing can bring out the raw truth in a situation and help you to analyse your feelings and understand why situations make you feel so bad. It can also help to put things in perspective, by enabling you to focus on the challenges you're facing and take a balanced look at your life.

With writing therapy, you can work through emotions, without fear of judgment or of igniting an inflammatory reaction from those who may not see things in quite the same way. There's no need to share your writing, but obviously you can if you want to. Some people find that burning their writing is a symbolic way of putting the past behind them and saying, "now it's gone".

Richard Pelzer, the brother of David, the most abused child in America, said that writing his book was therapeutic. It's a way of addressing feelings of mistreatment or abandonment and working through what happened. It can be very beneficial, and can help you see different perspectives, which may provide a greater sense of understanding too.

In times of economic recession and government cuts, where access to traditional therapies is at an all time premium, writing is free and accessible.

At the age of 19, while I was in recovery from a serious health challenge, I wrote a book about the experience. Despite some really encouraging feedback from Hodder and Stoughton, I had real confidence issues and their rejection made me abandon it, but the writing process itself was very therapeutic.

In 2005, researchers Baikie and Wilhelm, published a paper entitled 'Emotional and physical health benefits of expressive writing' in the medical journal, 'Advances in Psychiatric Treatment'. Their work looked at the numerous studies published on the topic of writing as therapy, and found that for most people, writing about your painful experiences for just 15 to 20 minutes a day, for three to five days, can help to improve your emotional wellbeing.

The therapeutic writing experience may be upsetting in the short term, but it provides a release that is beneficial to the writer in the longer term. The long-term benefits of therapeutic writing include lower stress levels, improved immunity, lower blood pressure, better physical health, and a sense of wellbeing. It may also reduce the risk of depression and post-traumatic avoidance behaviour. In addition, the research shows that the process may increase a writer's chance of finding employment, reduce their absenteeism at work, improve their memory, improve their grades at school, and improve their performance in sports. It's really quite remarkable how effective therapeutic writing can be.

So there's a clear therapeutic benefit, and perhaps a commercial one, in being able to express your deepest feelings on paper. Dozens of modern writers have delved deep into their pasts to write memoirs of their experiences. Their stories resonate with readers and a buoyant market for these stories continues to thrive.

In the abstract of their research findings, Baikie and Wilhelm wrote: "Writing about traumatic, stressful or emotional events has been found to result in improvements in both physical and psychological health, in non-clinical and clinical populations. In the expressive writing paradigm, participants are asked to write about such events for 15–20 minutes on 3–5 occasions. Those who do so generally have significantly better physical and psychological outcomes compared with those who write about neutral topics."

According to Smyth, 1998, a drug that could achieve the same benefits as writing therapy would be regarded as a "major medical advance".

However, it's important to note that there were certain groups of traumatised individuals where writing about their experiences was detrimental to their health. Therapeutic writing should be conducted with careful attention to its benefits - or lack of - in relation to the individual response, and if the individual is severely traumatised, it would be better conducted under the guidance of a medical professional. Read more: http://apt.rcpsych.org/content/11/5/338 .full

In recent times I've written articles about people who have overcome huge health challenges - a lady who had surgery for a brain tumour, and a man who was suddenly blinded, yet managed to live a full and active life. There's a real appetite for triumph over adversity stories in both book and magazine publishing, so if you have a tale to tell, get it down on paper. It might be a commercial success, and it might be therapeutic too!

Chapter 31
A freelance writer's life

This chapter takes a look at some of the aspects of a writer's life that you'll no doubt be familiar with, and perhaps some that you're not. Life as a freelance writer is rarely boring, and hopefully this chapter reflects some of the remarkable quirks of the freelance writing profession.

The cliquey writers' group

Writing is naturally a lonesome occupation and after nine months of doing it full time, I felt that I'd spent too much time on my own. I needed more of a social life, so I joined my local writers' group, hoping to meet like-minded people and further my writing career. The website assured me of a friendly welcome and the first meeting lived up to this claim with polite smiles and introductions. But within a few months I was having trouble getting beyond that polite 'hello'. They'd usually rush off to speak to someone else.

By April I'd received a book contract and was really excited. I was bursting to tell people, but the cliquey atmosphere prevailed and I left the April meeting without having told a single soul! I was starting to wonder why I bothered with the group at all. I wasn't learning much from the meetings and I wasn't making friends.

In a last ditch attempt to engage with people there, I decided to offer my services to the committee, suggesting I could work on the newsletter and deliver a talk on my new book. The chair wasn't interested. He turned me down flat, saying that the members were only interested in fiction. I only had one meaningful conversation with anyone in the group all year and was on the verge of giving up!

However, never one to be easily defeated, I decided to give it another year, and paid my dues. I'm glad I did because things turned around in the second year. I volunteered to read some work at a manuscript evening and when people heard a little about what I was doing, they started to show interest. Members started talking to me and I was even asked to do that talk!

So the moral of the story, is to persevere. Perhaps if your writing group is cliquey too, they just need time to get to know you. Offer to help with things and reach out to other new members if you can identify them. I've since joined the committee and, dare I say it, made a few friends!

My day in court
A few years ago, my husband and I were issued with a court order to defend ourselves against an accusation of negligence, after a young lad claimed that he had tripped over a pipe that was protruding from the pavement outside our house. It was an opportunistic suit, brought to court by a no-win-no-fee solicitor and it was the first we'd heard of the incident.

What relevance has this to writers? The experience heightened my awareness of the costs and implications of being dragged through the courts, even when you're innocent. The judge threw the case out of court after hearing the plaintiff's testimony. My husband and I were vindicated, but the case still took many hours of defence planning, paperwork, significant cost, and travel. We both had to take time off work to defend the case.

I try hard not to upset anyone in my writing because the last thing I want is another court case. It's something you might like to think about if you're ever writing something that might offend someone!

The whole experience was horrendous. It took over a year to get to court, during which time, we were constantly bombarded with demands on our time to prepare our defence, and it pushed our stress levels up through the roof. We are not used to being sued!

Fortunately, the case was covered by our home insurance, which was a huge relief. They put a £30,000 budget aside for our defence. Crazily, the offending obstacle wasn't our pipe and it wasn't on our land. It belonged to the gas supply company, who eventually moved it - although dozens of similar pipes still line the road! It's normal in that part of the UK.

We never actually got to present our full defence to the judge because the plaintiff's testimony was so unreliable that the case was dismissed following cross examination. His story was full of holes and inconsistencies.

It was a relief. However by then, the trial had put us through months of turmoil, sleepless nights, and the only upside, was that we were fully insured for the legal fees. However, there were still costs to us that were not fully reimbursed, even though the judge ruled in our favour: these costs included considerable time, considerable travel, and spiralling insurance costs, which doubled as a result of the claim.

So this leads me onto a point about writing and the law of libel. While strictly speaking, you can say what you want about people as long as it's true, the reality is that if they want to challenge what you have written in court under libel laws, you could be looking at a large defence bill, and more if you cannot prove that your words were true and are vindicated.

There are also considerable other time and cost implications of being sued. It's emotionally draining. Even if you win the case, you may well be out of pocket, as not all costs are automatically reimbursed.

That's why, as a writer, I steer clear of anything too controversial. I don't want to be hauled through the courts for libel, defamation, or damaging someone's business or reputation in a way that is unlawful.

I'm not in this business to dig dirt - I'll leave that to the publications who have sizable legal departments and defence budgets to match.

As a freelance writer you can get writers' professional indemnity insurance if you're worried about the risks of legal action.

Professional indemnity insurance

Insurance companies tend to consider writing as a high risk occupation, so you can't get professional indemnity insurance cheaply. From their perspective, you could write anything in newspapers published around the world and online that might be offensive, especially if you have insurance to protect you. Before you know it, you're in court up on a charge of libel.

The risk depends on what areas of journalism you're working in, but for peace of mind, professional indemnity insurance is worth considering. It covers you for libel claims, copyright infringement and other risks that writers may face during their career.

Imaging Insurance is the only insurer I've come across who is able to cover writers working for publications across the world, whose commissioned work sometimes goes unpublished for long periods of time, even years.

www.imaginginsurance.co.uk/writers.html

A journey of self-discovery

Writers' groups and court cases aside, becoming a full-time professional writer has brought dramatic change to my life, challenged my outlook, created new interests, and developed new skills. But most of all, it has helped me discover the real me. For years I felt crushed by other people's expectations about how I should look and behave, what I should think, where I should work, and what ambitions I should have (and not have).

As a full-time writer I feel free from these constraints and can finally just be myself, which is a wonderful experience. I can work the way I like, keep the hours I like, have whatever processes in place that I like, and write about things that I like. It's not all plain sailing and I still have to do jobs that are dull or uninspiring, but they enable me to do the jobs that I love and to live the lifestyle of a freelance writer, which is a great feeling.

I've also learnt a lot since I started writing for a living: about history and travel, and about publishing as an industry! It's fascinating to finally experience the quirks and annoyances of the industry that I strived to enter for so many years.

I've developed photography skills since starting my writing career and invested in some decent equipment because photographs are so important for some features. My latest acquisition is HDR Software, which offers a simple way to add drama and texture to my photos in a way that beats traditional photo-editing. I love the creative side of this business.

In the last few weeks I've been writing about lemurs, a lady who left an investment bank to become a zoo keeper, and I've been writing about the industrial revolution. It's been interesting. I've learnt about endangered species and conservation programmes, about the money-culture in an investment bank, and about the history of industrial growth in England during the 18th and 19th centuries.

Writing is a great way of learning new things, exploring new ideas, and expressing yourself creatively. What I write about is largely dictated by commissions from editors, which in turn is driven by what they think their readers are interested in. But obviously, I'm drawn towards the publications that print things I'm interested in, so the work is usually stimulating and enjoyable.

Being a freelance writer is a unique lifestyle, to which you need to be very committed. The variety of work is immense, the creative buzz is exhilarating, and submitting your work for publication provides a feel good factor all of its own. Then finally seeing your work in print.... it's all good.

The downside is that being on your own all day can be a bit lonely, even depressing if you're feeling low. So it makes sense to get out there and meet like-minded friends. Seeking support from a writers' circle, photography club, or other group of like-minded individuals can help to keep you smiling, and joining social networks of writers online can also be beneficial in keeping your spirits up, and giving you a well-earned break from your work occasionally!

Writing for a living has been a radical career change, because I work for myself now. I don't have to commute any more. I can be creative and write about the things I enjoy, and I can work the hours I like. I get paid on results not on process. Having bosses interfering with process used to really get my goat! I love being my own boss and I'm good at what I do. I also learn a lot more from researching topics for articles than I ever learnt in a conventional job. It's been a fascinating journey.

Writing is a vocation for many people, whether they make money at it or not. Writing can bring a sense of escapism, relief, or take you into another world. It can help you express yourself creatively and improve your literary skills.

If your dream is to write, stick with it. Solid determination and a passion for your writing work, will help to open doors.

Good luck!

Writers' Resources

This section is a collection of useful resources for writers, to help with finding work, training, conferences, or simply for inspiration!

Some of these opportunities are UK based (.co.uk), and others are worldwide (.com). They are a selection of the opportunities and are not definitive. Search more widely for more options in your own locality.

Writers' handbooks
The Writers and Artists Yearbook in the UK:
www.writersandartists.co.uk
The Australian Writers' Marketplace: www.awmonline.com.au
The Writers Market in the USA: www.writersmarket.com

Online job boards for writers
www.elance.com
www.guru.com
http://jobs.theguardian.com/jobs/media/
www.journalism.co.uk
www.holdthefrontpage.co.uk
www.gorkanajobs.co.uk/jobs/journalist
www.indeed.co.uk/Journalism-jobs

Journalism courses
www.nctj.com
www.guardian.co.uk/guardian-masterclasses/about-masterclasses
www.journalism.co.uk/vocational-skills-study/s43
www.bjtc.org.uk
www.city.ac.uk/arts-social-sciences/journalism/city-journalism-courses
www.sheffield.ac.uk/journalism
www.writersbureau.com

Writers' groups
Don't be a lonely writer. Writers' groups can provide feedback and support that make you feel part of a community, and help you to make new friends. They can egg you on, help you grow as a writer, and give you confidence. This is particularly helpful if others around you fail to understand what writing means to you, and are dismissive of your writing ambitions. Search online for a writers group in your local area. I am a member of Chiltern Writers: www.chilternwriters.org

Online communities for writers

www.writerscafe.org
www.writers-online.co.uk
www.scribophile.com
www.greatwriting.co.uk
www.writers-network.com
www.youngwritersonline.net
www.completelynovel.com
www.linkedin.com/groups
www.facebook.com/groups/the.writers.bureau
www.facebook.com/groups/ukpress

Membership associations

National Union of Journalists: www.nuj.org.uk
Society of Authors: www.societyofauthors.net
Author's Guild USA: www.authorsguild.org
National Writers' Union USA: www.nwu.org
The American Society of Journalists and Authors: www.asja.org

Websites for hooks and inspiration

Latest science news: www.sciencedaily.com
Significant dates in British history: www.information-britain.co.uk/famousdates.php
What happened in history on any given day: www.datesinhistory.com
Holidays around the world: www.earthcalendar.net
Bank holidays, and other notable dates: www.bankholidaydates.co.uk

Publishers and Agents

Cape Open Submissions: www.vintage-books.co.uk/capesubmissions
MacMillan New Writing: www.panmacmillan.com/imprints
Authonomy: www.authonomy.com
Writers' and Artists' Yearbook: www.writersandartists.co.uk

Self publishing

https://kdp.amazon.com/
www.nookpress.com/ebooks
www.kobo.com/writinglife
www.smashwords.com
www.lulu.com
www.lightningsource.com

Blogging Sites
www.blogspot.com
https://wordpress.org/

Conferences
www.southernwriters.co.uk
www.greatwriting.org.uk
www.writersworkshop.co.uk/events.html
www.newpages.com/writing-conferences
www.pwcwriters.org

Writers' Wheel Magazine
Writers' Wheel Magazine is a free online magazine for writers, published by John Hunt Publishing. You can download copies on the links below. Save the PDF files to your C drive. Then the pages will load more quickly when you want to read them.
www.issuu.com/writerswheel

Useful blogs
My Writing Life: www.susiekearley.blogspot.co.uk
Womag Writers: www.womagwriter.blogspot.com
Mistakes Writers Make: www.mistakeswritersmake.blogspot.co.uk
Simon Whaley's Tutor Blog: www.simonwhaleytutor.blogspot.com

Other useful websites
www.absolutewrite.com
www.goodreads.com
www.writerunboxed.com
www.worldwidefreelance.com
www.successify.net
http://royal.pingdom.com/2013/01/16/internet-2012-in-numbers

Follow Susie Kearley on Social Media
Facebook: www.facebook.com/susie.kearley.writer
Twitter: www.twitter.com/susiekearley

Freelance Writing on Health, Food and Gardens
by Susie Kearley

In 2011 Susie Kearley quit a 15 year marketing career to start up as a freelance writer in the middle of a recession. In this book, she shares how, in under two years, she went from being an aspirational rookie, to working for some of the biggest names in publishing.

She explains how:
* she built up valuable contacts from nothing;
* she used her nutrition qualifications and background in natural health to spur her career forward;
* she generated numerous feature ideas from single opportunities;
* she sold articles on health, food and gardening topics to diverse and unexpected markets;
* her unrelenting perseverance and tenacity came good in the end, despite numerous obstacles;
* she challenged those who said she would never succeed and proved them wrong.

This book is inspirational. It provides valuable tips to get you started in writing for the health, food and gardening markets, and has wider relevance to other fields of journalism.

Interviews with other writers - all working in the health, food and gardening markets - give superb insight into the highlights and challenges that each of them have faced in this field of work. The book features interviews with some well-known writers, and with others who are still building their reputation, including: Amanda Hamilton, celebrity nutritionist and health writer; Jackie Lynch, nutritionist and health writer; Nick Baines, travel writer focusing on food topics; Sue Ashworth, food and cookery writer; John Negus, gardening writer; Helen Riches, garden designer and writer. Each of these professionals offers their own hints for getting published in their specialist markets.

Susie provides humorous accounts of the obstacles she faced, as well as tips on how to write a winning pitch, how to market yourself as a writer, and how to avoid legal issues.

Printed in Great Britain
by Amazon